CW00587941

Writers of Wales

Editors
MEIC STEPHENS   R. BRINLEY JONES

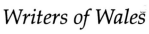

Leslie Norris

GLYN JONES

University of Wales Press

Cardiff 1997

821.914
J

I

*My great-grandfather, born Merthyr 1810, was a horse
contractor living in Mountain Hare - the house with the yard
around it still stands - conveniently near Ffair y Waun, that
famous horse fair dating from the thirteenth century. What
lucky boys we were to have been brought up in Merthyr.*
(Glyn Jones, in a letter, 8 March 1967)

Like his great-grandfather, Glyn Jones was also born
in Merthyr Tydfil; not, it is true, in Mountain Hare,
but only a few miles down the mountainside. Above
Mountain Hare the moorland is still desolate and
largely unspoiled. From certain places there it is
possible to look right into the heart of the town and
yet be completely alone. A boy living in that place,
particularly a boy who was to be a poet, could
see with delight the solitary birds and animals of
the inhospitable hills, curlew, fox, ring ouzel, and
twenty minutes later be scuffling with his friends in
the High Street. This is true of many south Wales
towns, but nowhere is it as dramatically true as it is
in Merthyr Tydfil, at the foothills of the Brecon
Beacons; and the sharp division between town and
country is to be found in most of Glyn Jones's work,
often carrying a symbolic emphasis, as we shall see.

When Glyn Jones was born, in 1905, the town still
held some of its splendour. It was still comparatively
prosperous, and full of astonishing vigour. Something of its intellectual flavour is described in the
early pages of THE DRAGON HAS TWO TONGUES, those

pages Glyn Jones called his 'Autobiography', although they are a loving celebration of the place as much as anything, and a quietly proud narrative of the lives of Glyn Jones's ancestors in the town. His pedigree is impeccable. His mother's family were established in the valley long before its industrialization; his father's people, leaving their farm in Llanybri in Carmarthenshire, came to settle in the growing town in the early years of the last century. Almost alone among its chroniclers, Glyn Jones has written of *the considerable intellectual ferment and artistic activity* that were part of the life of Merthyr Tydfil, of *the eisteddfodau, and literary, musical and Welsh cultural societies* which flourished there. His grandfather, David William Jones, insurance agent and missionary manqué, was part of this society, since he was also the noted poet 'Llwch-Haiarn'. For the young Glyn Jones, literature, music and philosophy were part of life.

'Llwch-Haiarn', of course, wrote in Welsh, for much the greater part of that cultural activity was performed and discussed in the Welsh language. *I was born*, Glyn Jones wrote, . . . *into a Welsh-speaking family, so that my own first language was Welsh*. It was the pressure of the growing anglicization of the speech of the town, containing as it did not only Welsh people, but English, Irish, Scots and Spaniards, that caused the boy to lose *the ability and desire to speak Welsh*. No Welsh was spoken at school. Of his grammar school, Cyfarthfa Castle School, first built as a mansion for the Crawshays, Glyn Jones commented bitterly, *it was the most anglicising influence of my life*. It was his belief that the language a writer uses during adolescence, *the language of his awakening*, is likely to be used for his creative work. This may very well be so, and would seem to be true in his individual example. But within a few years of Glyn Jones's time at the Castle School, Welsh was a flourishing discipline there and eisteddfodau were held each year. By that time Glyn Jones knew he was a writer. At St Paul's College, Cheltenham, where he went to train as a teacher, he was about to fall under the spell of D. H. Lawrence. Returning from college to teach in Cardiff two things were to mark the impressionable young man: the appalling poverty of the children he taught, and the study of contemporary literature he undertook at this time. Of the first he wrote movingly in THE DRAGON HAS TWO TONGUES:

When a child in my class was ill I would sometimes go to his home or room after school to see how he was progressing, and what I witnessed on these visits, the squalor, the overcrowding, the degradation, the poverty, I have never forgotten.

From these years, perhaps, may spring the extraordinary generosity and tolerance he showed towards the poor and malformed who appear often in the pages of his prose. Children are shown frequently as vulnerable, tragic and innocently heroic. Trefor, one of the children in Glyn Jones's novel, THE VALLEY, THE CITY, THE VILLAGE, is *a passionate micher* and wears a *choirboy's cassock cut off at the waist for a jacket.* His life is hard, for his mother is a widow, her house always full of steam from the washing she took in, and Trefor *had to gather nettles for making small beer or collect horse-dung in an old pram.* Yet none of these circumstances is worth commenting on. Trefor is valuable as a person, his humanity is perfect, he *had the best shooting cymal* (knuckle-joint) *in school for playing marbles.* Similarly,

3

in the same work, we meet the O'Learys, *a lovely family of seven or eight children all wild as bears and with no parents.* One of them, Mikey, *had a withered arm and the smallest had an iron on his leg,* but we are left with the impression that neither child was at all put out by such disability. Climbing all over their curtainless house or their garden that grew only holes, the O'Learys sing through a paragraph on page 21 and never appear again.

During this time Glyn Jones read widely. Although he liked Joyce, Wyndham Lewis, Roy Campbell, Aldous Huxley and Virginia Woolf, it was D. H. Lawrence whose work he loved. *My literary hero then was D. H. Lawrence,* he wrote, and he showed how deeply he identified with the older writer in a passage from THE DRAGON HAS TWO TONGUES:

Lawrence had been a young teacher at one time like myself, he had been brought up in a mining area near a countryside of exceptional natural beauty as I had been, his family were Congregationalists and mine were the Welsh equivalent, namely Independents . . . it was the work of Lawrence, dealing with an environment so like in many ways the one I had been brought up in myself, that first made me think of writing.

Young writers are, of course, quick to recognize, even if unconsciously, those members of their craft from whom they can learn, who have used already the qualities not yet mature in the budding artist. Glyn Jones seems to have detected very early what in D. H. Lawrence was to be useful for his own practice. Not only did he see that it was possible to use for literature an environment so like that which Lawrence had used, but that *the brilliance of the imagery in Lawrence, the vividness of his language and*

4

the deep feeling . . . were also properties which he himself possessed. By what must have seemed the most happy omen, *the year 1931, in which I bought the two volumes of Lawrence's collected poems*, saw his *own first poems appear in print*. Unlike Lawrence, Glyn Jones remained true to his early material, writing always of Wales and the Welsh, but there are, nevertheless, deep points of resemblance between the work of the two men.

At first the influence of Lawrence was very marked, and perhaps we ought to say that the example has also been positive in ways other than those of style and material. It may well have been, for instance, that had it not been for the fact that Lawrence wrote in prose as well as poetry, Glyn Jones might have remained a poet only. We might never have had the novels and short stories. It is easy to recognize in 'Marwnad', a poem from Glyn Jones's first collection, POEMS (1939), both the manner and the matter of Lawrence:

> *The little oil-lamp burns between us;*
> *It is made of blue glass;*
> *Beside the bare table we sit waiting*
> *For the night to pass.*
>
> ('Marwnad')

> *The new red houses spring like plants*
> *In level rows*
> *Of reddish herbage that bristles and slants*
> *Its square shadows.*
> (Lawrence, 'Flat suburbs, S.W., in the morning')

'Marwnad' is a poem in which a miner's wife, her husband killed underground and lying in the next room, wonders when her *pains will come upon her*.

5

Such a poem, spoken from the woman's point of view and in a woman's voice, is typical of Lawrence and unlike anything Glyn Jones was to write later. There are, however, several similar pieces in Jones's COLLECTED POEMS (1996), among the early poems Meic Stephens has included in this sensitively edited and important work. They resemble such poems of Lawrence's as 'The Collier's Wife', or 'Violets', or 'The Drained Cup'. Jones's early story, 'I Was Born in the Ystrad Valley', is also recognizably, as far as style is concerned, influenced by Lawrence.

Yet there is a sense in which such influence is superficial. Valuable as Lawrence's work was as an example, circumstances combined to make Glyn Jones's own writing turn in another direction. First, he discovered the poems of G. M. Hopkins, in whose lines he recognized again the kind of brilliant imagery he so admired in Lawrence. (It is, perhaps, significant that both Hopkins and Lawrence were competent painters, their imagery predominantly visual. This was also true of Glyn Jones. He said of himself,

I had always shown some aptitude for and much interest in drawing and painting, and in the circumstances it was very much the wish of my mother that I should go to an art school . . . but I opted for a teachers' training college . . .)

Now, at a time when he was beginning to write, he met in Hopkins the work of a poet who had studied Welsh poetry, admired its complex forms, and used his knowledge and admiration in his own work. Within a short time, in 1932, Glyn Jones began to read for himself in Welsh literature and from this his voice was made complete. Speaking of his experience when reading such poets as Dafydd ap Gwilym for the first time, he said:

All of what I read I did not completely understand, because after twenty years of indifference my Welsh was uncertain and limited; but I could take in enough to be swept off my feet by the unfamiliar music of the cywyddau, *by the brilliance of their imagery and by their sharp response to the visual beauty of the world.*

These were clearly the qualities of his own work. He was completing a process of self-recognition when he identified his own strengths in the work of his mentors.

One result of his awakening to the work in Welsh of his great predecessors has been that he was sometimes sad, almost a little guilty, that his education left him so badly equipped to write his work in Welsh. He wrote in THE DRAGON HAS TWO TONGUES:

What I was quite incapable of doing was myself writing prose or poetry that seemed to me of any value or distinction at all in Welsh . . . every line of poetry that has risen unsought and unexpectedly in my mind, the words of every image and description, almost every striking and individual word, have all been English.

Yet this significant passage contains more, possibly, than it seems to say. It tells us that Glyn Jones saw the creative process as largely intuitive and unconscious, every line arising *unsought and un-expected*, and that these were qualities he valued. His Welsh was good enough for him to have been invited to judge Welsh prose competitions at the National Eisteddfod, and had he been a conscious rather than an intuitive artist it would certainly have been good enough for him to have used for his creative work. But intuitively and unconsciously he used the *striking and individual* English words he manipulated so well. *I fancy words* he said in his poem 'Merthyr': it is not entirely a loss that the words he fancied were English.

If, then, there seems something paradoxical in his use of English as his chosen literary medium, it might almost be symptomatic of the deeper schism, the more elemental contradiction that is at the heart of much of Glyn Jones's work, particularly the prose. He had himself recognized the two worlds of his life, that of the town with all its imperfections and that of the paradisial countryside. In the Wales of Glyn Jones's vision, the language of the town is always English, a vigorous and colloquial English maybe, and sometimes enriched by an exotic Welsh word or construction, but English. Apart from the energy and invention of the writer's ebullient style, it is recognizably the language of the Taff Valley. The language of the country, however, is Welsh. Although reported as English, its rhythms are noticeably slower, deeper and more innocent than those of the town. Nearly all that is unhappy occurs in the peeling streets of Ystrad, Jones's town since he started to write and an obvious *nom de guerre* for Merthyr Tydfil, whereas the countryside, whether it is the bare nobility of the north Glamorgan and Breconshire hills or the landscape near Llansteffan (these are the two areas of his country heaven), is the scene of all that is idyllic, as well as the only sort of place in which his characters can achieve the beauty and self-knowledge of which they are capable. The grotesques live in the town, but the country characters have a real and simple dignity. Again, and in this too Jones was not unlike Lawrence, true poetry was all on the side of the fields and hills, since only among them is there time for true observation. Life in Ystrad was surprising and violent, beyond the control of anyone who lived there, but in the villages and little farms a traditional rhythm, older than time almost, gave purpose and a sense of order to its inhabitants.

Yet, in the end, it is to the town that Glyn Jones returned. He makes this explicit in the lines from 'Merthyr' in which he asked God to allow him to die not *behind that county borough / Known as Merthyr in Glamorganshire,* but *inside that county borough,* shabby and battered though it is. He knew, and told us of, the spectacular beauty of the Beacon slopes, but at the end he wished to lie down among his friends, *the legendary walkers and actors* of his town, and *the memory of neighbours, worthies, relatives.* He delighted in their individuality, seeing in people the true revelation of divinity. Two quotations are enough to prove this point, both from THE VALLEY, THE CITY, THE VILLAGE:

To me my granny was always a warm and visionary being. Sometimes, the whole sky ablaze, and the crimson sunball dissolving hot as rosin upon the hill-top, a tall black figure seemed to float out of that bonfire as though riding a raft of illumination. Her heavy progress was laborious, her shoulders rose and fell against the dazzling hump of hill-crest radiance with the rock of a scale-beam. She shepherded her rolling shadow down the slope; returning from the prayer-meeting she wore over her vast flesh her long black boat-cloak, with the brass buttons like a dramatic row of drawer-knobs down the front of her . . . Then, as she turned to the cut sun and the after-glow, her lined face became lit up, illuminated as though from within like a rock of clear crystal; her opaque body glowed, momentary

9

starlight inhabited her glistening form. And I, shouting at the sight of her, reached her side with singing limbs, she was my radiant granny, my glossy one, whose harsh fingers lay gently and sweet as a harp-hand upon my curls.

In the last pages of the novel, a vision of this impressive woman speaks out in strong condemnation of those Welshmen who do not know that the history of Wales is the history of its small people.

You shall learn concerning your ancestors, the taeogion *of the princely* cywyddau; *you shall read how you were borne off to Ulster in the slave-ships, crowded among the yellow hunting-dogs; you shall learn of the centuries of your labouring, a traverser of farmlands, despoiled and plundered, the victim of the merciless princes and their conquerors alike, your barley-crops burnt, your few sheep driven off . . . You were robbed on the toll-roads, fastened in stocks, evicted for exercising a legal right, imprisoned, deported, punished for speaking the language of your fathers . . . You are the third generation of your family to read books. You are the second to live without the fear of poverty and old age. You are the first to choose the work you wish to do . . .*

Glyn Jones was perhaps the nearest thing the Anglo-Welsh had to a Man of Letters. He wrote poems, short stories, novels, reviews, art criticism, social history, radio scripts. He was curious about every aspect of human activity, about people he forgot nothing. The *taeogion* of the princely *cywyddau* were as real to him as that blind man of his youth, who sat every day outside Merthyr Market, reading aloud from his great Braille Bible as the passers-by dropped pennies into his hat. Tolerant, fantastically observant, delighted by every manifestation of human idiosyncracy, he sat alert in his world,

Hopkins's poems and, even more strongly, his absorbed study of the *cywyddau*. But Thomas's example served remarkably well to intensify and strengthen the development of a new area for Glyn Jones. From then on, although the bulk of his work was still written in the first person, only rarely is the narrator deeply involved in the action of a story or novel. Rather is he the concerned and sympathetic observer, the friend or relative of the main character, near enough to be at the scene of events, but not to take part in them. Thus he has time to look at everything, describe everything, even, very often, to pick leisurely through the bag of dazzling treasures which form Glyn Jones's characteristic vocabulary.

Although this change of direction happened early in Jones's career as a writer of short stories, it was nevertheless an important one. Apart from the fact that it enabled his prose and his poetry to follow closely related paths, allowing him to use in his stories the images and rhythms of his poems, and affording him opportunities of combining the tragic and the humorous in a way he made his own, it was not easy for him to abandon a political attitude. Any sensitive young man living in south Wales in the thirties was almost forced to become a politician, to look for political causes and cures for the vast human despoliation of the time. Glyn Jones was only too well aware of this. He had, moreover, lived in Merthyr Tydfil, the most radical of towns; he was accustomed to considering the great sweep of political movements as the marvellous orators of the time described them:

My abiding interest, he wrote in a letter, *in politics started in the old Skating Rink in Merthyr, and in Thomastown Park, listening to Tom Mann, Mrs Despard, Mrs Bruce Glazier etc. Another of the great free shows to be enjoyed on all hands in Merthyr then.*

It is obvious that he was as interested in rhetoric as he was in polemic, but it was still an astonishing act of recognition which led him away from the road his contemporaries – Auden, Day-Lewis and Orwell – were all bravely marching along, and to accompany Dylan Thomas on what seemed then so unfashionable a journey.

Shortly after his meeting with Dylan Thomas, and still in 1934, the two young men wrote to Caradoc Evans, asking for permission to visit him. It is easy now to see reasons for their admiration. Evans's mastery of form, his precise economy, his scalding denunciation of hypocrisy in high places, all are more clearly visible now than they were in 1934 when the thickets of his inflammatory reputation tended to obscure the quality of his work. He was then fifty-six, *a hated and notorious figure in Wales, a blasphemer and a mocker, a derider of our religion,* wrote Glyn Jones. But he was also a considerable artist, one whose stories Glyn Jones, almost in spite of himself, *read with considerable admiration.* They were stories very firmly set in Wales. The sense of Cardiganshire, not necessarily a Cardiganshire of which Glyn Jones would have approved, but a county rather like it would be if its inhabitants were stripped of all kindness and generosity, its fields sour and blasted, its chapels ruled by the devil, was recognizable and strong. This too Glyn Jones needed and used; he accepted the sharp detail the older writer used, he adapted the physical sense of person and place for his own purposes. Some of Glyn Jones's vivid

16

preoccupation with the physical appearance of his people seems to date from this time, although his technique was quite unlike that of Caradoc Evans. Evans would strike out a fantastic picture in a few superbly economic strokes. Glyn Jones dwelt with infinite care on the precise detail of a hand, a nose, the buttons on a dress. Where Evans was selective, Glyn Jones was inclusive. As the anonymous contributor to THE CONCISE ENCYCLOPAEDIA OF MODERN WORLD LITERATURE states in his admiring and perceptive article on Glyn Jones:

In these stories Glyn Jones uses, to great effect, his gift for irrelevance. The ability to be irrelevant, and at the same time to achieve form, is rare. But Glyn Jones does this. His irrelevance is significant because for him, fundamentally, nothing is irrelevant. Putrefaction is relevant, detail is important, beauty is not selective: the writer is not here to censor perception.

From these sources and others like them, but mostly from the recognition of his own gift and a growing mastery of his craft, came the stories in THE BLUE BED.

Reading now the reviews which attended the publication of THE BLUE BED, it is difficult to understand why Glyn Jones was not more generally recognized as the master of the short story he undoubtedly was. The extraordinary invention and energy of this early book were clearly welcomed, and the unusual promise of the writer was sensitively praised. H. E. Bates wrote in the old MORNING POST:

The stories in The Blue Bed *remind me of tapestries, intricately and sensitively woven; his words are deep-dyed threads, his figures remote and vague and yet not quite unreal. From the first page you perceive here an uncommon talent, prodigal but sure, sensuous but conscious, a man revelling in the luxury of words and yet having something fresh and powerful to declare. These stories are, by conventional standards, less like stories than prose poems. Mr Jones breaks the rules; huge paragraphs, verbose and meandering pages. Writing exclusively of Wales, he never shows us Wales realistically, with clarity; only a kind of dream country, poignant, tragic, always sensuous . . . you are conscious of the voice of an extraordinary writer finding both himself and his way. This is a first book produced out of a first phase, and it is a richly promising achievement.*

There were other firm messages of welcome: from Edwin Muir, who called the book *the work of a very remarkable writer*, from Richard Hughes, who contributed a long and enthusiastic review to the OBSERVER, from Humbert Wolfe, from Edward Garnett, who wrote forthrightly, *Glyn Jones is a genius.* Even those reviewers who began, *I would not call* [THE BLUE BED] *. . . a nice book* often ended up having written the highest praise – *. . . in sustained and nervous intensity some of these tales are the equal of the most ghastly exploits in* Lawrence's SEVEN PILLARS OF WISDOM, *but there is nothing in D.H. of the same name to touch them . . .*

Even in those ampler days, when reviewers were given space to spread themselves, so general and favourable a reception was very unusual. It is significant, too, that his most fervent supporters, those who saw most clearly Glyn Jones's intentions and recognized his achievement, were all writers themselves. He had gained the approval of his peers. Now, many years later, we can see that the influence of Lawrence, visible in 'I Was Born in the Ystrad Valley', is by no means obtrusive in the other stories and is, moreover, the reflection of a genuine affinity rather than the effect of anything approaching creative imitation.

THE BLUE BED is long out of print and of its nine stories only four are to be found in SELECTED SHORT STORIES (1971). These are 'Knowledge', a comparatively realistic and moving tale of the sensitive areas of loving misunderstanding between a young man and his wife; 'Wil Thomas', a macabre and very funny story of a one-eyed miner visited by the ghost of the local preacher; 'Eben Isaac', that marvellous story of the dead village baker; and, perhaps the finest, 'Cadi Hughes', the brief, fantastic fable of a just and eccentric God come to take one of his faithful. These are fine stories, full of splendid touches. Ifan Cariad, for example, dying of progressive gangrene, is described like this:

Most of the time he was lying sog after the dope the doctor was giving him daily to ease his pain. His face in a short time had become yellow as clay and tiny, hardly bigger than a hand, with his nose rising up tight in the middle like a plucked fowl's breastbone. They had cut his hair short for comfort, and it looked like the pile on black velvet or plush, and fitted like a cap on top of his little monkey-face.

('Cadi Hughes')

This passage is typical of the writing in all four of these early stories; simply constructed and seemingly artless, it is far more deliberate and designing than it appears. Beginning with the introduction of the curious word 'sog', used here as it is in south Wales to suggest a heavy, almost insensible condition, the dying man is removed further and further from humanity with every image; his face was no longer human, it was like clay, it was yellow,

19

it was like a hand; his hair was not natural; it was like velvet or plush; his nose, in the most macabre yet the most accurate of images, was like a dead chicken's breastbone. Already, *below the level of consciousness*, we are told there is no hope for Ifan Cariad. And, despite the homely properties of the writing, the accuracy of the observation, the exquisite arrangement of the detail and the brilliant precision of the imagery give to the paragraph something of the nature of poetry. And if 'Cadi Hughes' holds some echo of Glyn Jones's admiration for Caradoc Evans, as in this dialogue:

. . . one day near the end, he whispered, 'Cadi, give me something to eat.'

'Of course, little Ifan,' she said, humouring him. 'What will you have?'

'I'd like some of that dinner I can smell cooking.'

'Oh, you can't have that, little Ifan,' she said, 'that's the ham boiling, for the funeral.'

we can be assured that, generally speaking, the just get their reward in Glyn Jones's world, and that unkindness is rare and despised among his people.

Fine though these four early stories are, they nevertheless display an incomplete account of THE BLUE BED. Those which were omitted from the SELECTED STORIES, stories like 'The Blue Bed' itself, or 'The Kiss', are beautifully fluent and full of a serious and involved compassion. Glyn Jones's style was already clear and precise, not at all idiosyncratic. It was, in the best sense, a literary style, a written prose; it carried little evidence of the speaking voice of Glyn Jones, as later stories do. There is real anger in some of these stories, direct and outspoken; in

20

them Glyn Jones examined and condemned the inhumanity of the world in which he lived. If, in that way, they are untypical, they are still important, exemplifying an aspect of his compassion which Glyn Jones chose not to develop, or perhaps not to make public. (There are examples of vivid condemnation in some of his notes, and some sardonic lines among the newly published work in THE COLLECTED POEMS.) He could obviously have been a writer whose work was much more directly political and didactic.

That he chose another path is not an indication that he shut his eyes to injustice, or that he was unaware of the more unpleasant manifestations of contemporary life; in fact he was more clear-sighted than most artists. A vastly unjudging man, he was interested more in humanity than anything else, and his tolerance was a result of his understanding. Yet it is still possible to regret the loss of 'I Was Born in the Ystrad Valley', 'The Kiss', 'Eden Tree', 'The Blue Bed', and 'Porth-y-Rhyd'. The range in these stories, despite the similarity of background, was extraordinarily wide, moving from the rumbustious fancy of Glyn Jones's humour to the most delicate of still-life descriptions:

. . . all the bones pure white and dry, and chalky, but perfect without a crack or flaw anywhere. At the back, rising out of the beak, were twin domes like bubbles of thin bone, almost transparent, where the brain had been that fixed the tilt of the wings.

Small wonder that Hugh MacDiarmid, the great Scottish poet, having read that reconstruction of a bird's skull, was so impressed by it that he thought it his own, and published it, allowing its natural rhythms to fall into the shape of verse. Such a tribute, even if unconscious, bears witness to the extraordinary 'rightness', the sensuous clarity of Glyn Jones's prose. His stories are full of such small gems; hardly a page exists without lines as hard and clear.

And he was, despite MacDiarmid's tribute, not merely a writer's writer. At once lyrical and precise, highly individual yet immediate amd immensely accurate, he was, like those old politicians to whom he listened when young, an entertainer. He button-holes his reader, he is racy, charming, the surface of his prose glitters.

Pentrebach was a little farming village in the hills behind the Sidan bay, a couple of rows of white-washed cottages in a street sloping up to the top of a hill where there was a square with a pump in it. From here you could see the cut fields on the hills all round like sheets of green blotting paper among the tangled cables of the hedges, and on a clear day you could make out the sea, smooth as a slab of blue bag-leather in the distance. The village baker was a mean old chap called Eben Isaac . . .

It was the voice of the true storyteller. In that passage he demonstrates, too, the strength of his visual imagery. It is as if he had never read a line of literature, going unerringly for a simile that grew from his experience and the wish to communicate as completely as language will allow something palpable and concrete. So his fields are *like sheets of green blotting-paper,* the sea *smooth as a slab of blue bag-leather.* Such selection results in an unlikely relevance almost metaphysical in its novelty, the images bringing with them the authentic shock of novel and delighted recognition.

And if his world is lit by some perfect light in which every detail has the clarity we find in an early Italian painting, so that each object, whether of foreground or background is immaculately realized, then the same complete light surrounds his people. Against this clear world and in this light his people move, every wrinkle and hair definite and identifiable. (It is only fair to add that such a passion for the visible is an Anglo-Welsh characteristic. Similar examples might be found in the stories of Geraint Goodwin, Alun Lewis, Gwyn Thomas, Gwyn Jones etc. Professor Gwyn Jones has already noticed this; in his 'Language, Style and the Anglo-Welsh', he writes:

Of the Anglo-Welsh senses the visual is the early riser and the harder worker . . .

but even he is bound to add that it was specifically and especially true of Glyn Jones:

. . . if he describes a bulbous nose, we see, we do not squeeze it; if water, it laves the skin less than it makes rainbows in the lashes.

This is graceful and acute. But it should be stated that Glyn Jones's rhythms demonstrate that he also possessed a subtle and inventive ear. Perhaps his eye was used with more conscious artistry.)

Here is a Glyn Jones character stepping alive and dapper from one of the stories:

His father was a big tall man wearing pale spats, a white felt hat pushed on the side of his head and a thin grey suit with a collar to the waistcoat and a scarlet carnation in the button-hole. He was smoking a thin cigar like a pencil which he was using to point with, and which he kept passing from hand to hand as he

made jokes and explained things to Arthur and me, bending
down with his bright eyes close to mine and his breath smelling
of scented cachous. He had a gold band on one of his fingers
with a hailstone in it, and he laughed and talked all the time in a
rich-sounding way, showing a lot of gold in his big teeth. I
thought him lovely then, more beautiful than a mermaid, with
his mannish smell, and his handsome pink cheeks, and his thick
curly hair like grey tobacco.

The narrator is, of course, a boy. The character is
another boy's father, and here, in the exotic
strangeness of Mr Morgan, whose hands, hair, even
his waistcoat, are described in such loving detail, we
also learn by implication that the boy's own house is
quite unlike the house this man lives in, *his* father
ordinary and familiar. Mr Morgan is a minor
character in the story 'Bowen, Morgan and
Williams', if, that is, there are minor characters in
Glyn Jones's work. For him, nobody was unimportant and nothing was to be left out; yet this
passion for inclusiveness, his obsession with the
minutest details of appearance and behaviour, led
not to chaos but to clear, formal pattern, a sturdy
sense of form.

'Bowen, Morgan and Williams' is from THE WATER
MUSIC (1944), a collection of twelve short stories. Of
them, Glyn Jones wrote:

Dylan very early urged me to write short stories, and in 1937
my first collection, THE BLUE BED, appeared. In Llanstephan, I
think it was, the summer of 1938. I mentioned to Caitlin
Thomas that I had started a second volume, a series of short
stories about childhood, or at least what was once known as
'enfance'. She seemed very surprised and told me that Dylan
had already started doing exactly the same thing. His were the

24

autobiographical stories which in 1940 appeared as PORTRAIT
OF THE ARTIST AS A YOUNG DOG. *My own stories were
collected into* THE WATER MUSIC *and published in 1944.*
(THE DRAGON HAS TWO TONGUES)

In its way, this is a most interesting passage, stating as it
does that Dylan Thomas's stories were autobiographical while implying that Glyn's stories were drawn less
directly from experience. A number of Glyn's critics
have suggested that his work in THE WATER MUSIC is
lightly   disguised   autobiography,   and   natives   of
Merthyr Tydfil can very often give a local habitation
and a name to the scenes of his events. But we must be
very cautious before we discount the alchemy of his
imagination. THE WATER MUSIC stories are very unlike
those in PORTRAIT OF THE ARTIST AS A YOUNG DOG. They
differ widely in time, place and style; 'The Apple-Tree',
'The Saviour' and 'The Wanderer', written in a highly
charged poetic prose, are not unlike the stories Dylan
Thomas included in THE MAP OF LOVE. 'The Four-
Loaded Man' and 'The Little Grave' are almost folk
tales; 'Explosion' is the realistic story of a child in
school when news of an explosion in the pit affects one
of his friends; 'An Afternoon at Ewa Shad's' is the tale
of a suicide attempt as seen by a child, and so on. Of the
twelve stories in THE WATER MUSIC, six are written in
the first person, and it is significant that these are the
stories most clearly based on reality. 'Bowen, Morgan
and Williams' and 'The Water Music', the last two
stories in the collection and which deal with children
as they reach adolescence, are not only the most
successful stories included, but clearly point the way to
Glyn Jones's novels. Not all twelve stories found a
place in SELECTED SHORT STORIES, 'The Apple-Tree', 'The
Wanderer', 'The Little Grave' and 'Explosion' being left
out.

25

It is not surprising that Glyn Jones wrote so much about children and childhood. He had been for some time a schoolmaster and remained one for forty years (*conscientious, I'm afraid, not dedicated,* is how he described himself) with ample opportunity for observing boys. In all his work, even in his novel THE LEARNING LARK, in which he took a swing at several fairly easy targets, he never was anything but sympathetic to children, understanding their difficulties in an adult society, aware of their sad lack of dignity, sensitive towards the curious set of values by which they organize their lives.

THE WATER MUSIC, then, is a more homogeneous collection than its predecessor; partly because it is a book about childhood, partly because it is stylistically more uniform than THE BLUE BED, and partly because the arrangement of the stories shows a progress in time and a deepening in the use of significant detail. 'The Apple-Tree' and 'The Saviour', the first two stories, are rather general in effect, but 'Bowen, Morgan and Williams' and 'The Water Music' are particular and individual in detail. These stories are also linked in that the characters are the same, boys at the grammar school in Ystrad, and friends in that unquestioning and perfect way which is made only in adolescence, made then and lasting for life. The combination of these two stories is strange, a combination of affection, wild humour and the ecstatic, almost obsessed poetry which go to make up the adolescent's inner world:

I praise him for his endless fertility and inventiveness, in that he stripes, shades, patches and stipples every surface of his creation in his inexhaustable designing, leaves no stretch of water unmarked, no sand or snow-plain without the relief of interfering stripe, shadow or cross-hatch, no spread of pure sky but he deepens it from the pallor of its edges to its vivid zenith. I praise him that he is never baulked, never sterile, never repetitious.

There is praise for him in my heart and in my flesh pulled over my heart, there is praise for him in my pain and in my enjoying. I show my praise for him in the unnecessary skip of my walk, in my excessive and delighted staring, in the exuberance of my over-praise.

And when I dive I shall feel the ice of speed and praise him, the shock and tingle of the goldlaced pool and praise him, the chrism of golden sunshine poured on my drenching head and praise him.

I dive into the engulfing water praising him.

It is to the young that Glyn Jones gave many of the most important revelations. A child or a schoolboy can look at the terror and beauty of the world, and its humour too, with an innocence and candour that precludes judgement. So the dead putrid flesh of a collier can be beautiful because a brother's love makes it so, and a very small boy can watch the pathetic attempts of a failed suicide with un-recognizing fascination. Rosie Bowen, despite his ugliness, is loved as deeply and completely as the exquisite Arthur Trevelyan Vaughan Morgan, and for the same reason, his uniquely human condition:

Benja was a bit mis-shapen, he was short, thick-set and bull-necked with arms hanging down to his knees like an ape. His short powerful legs were bandy because he had broken both of them and he had a great wrinkled cone of ginger hair piled up on top of his head like coco-nut matting. His bottom jaw, covered with blond, unshaven cub-fur, stuck out beyond his top and his

*cheeks were red, but if you called him Rosie or Cochyn he would
punch you on the muscles. He had his best clothes on, an Eton
collar, a black coat and vest and striped trousers stinking of
tobacco, and a pair of button boots someone had ordered from his
father and never paid for. His father was a bootmaker and you
could always see the top of him showing above the green-painted
window of their shop . . .*

The adoption of a 'child's-eye view' meant that Glyn
Jones rejected, to some extent, a deliberately intellectual content in his stories, since judgement is an
intellectual task. He relied on a largely intuitive
approach, feeling and relishing the texture of his
sentences as if they were woven and coloured. (It is
in THE WATER MUSIC that we see the most obvious
manifestations of a tendency that was to become
more marked in the novels – a delight in words that
some critics found almost too bizarre.) This
deliberately intuitive method – he was not an
intuitive *artist*, nobody could have been more
concerned with his craft – enabled him to gain
compensating strengths. Like a child, he could
indulge in *excessive and delighted staring*, in *the
exuberance of over-praise*.

SELECTED SHORT STORIES (1971) contains some early
stories, eight from THE WATER MUSIC, and three,
'Jordan', 'The Boy in the Bucket' and 'It's not by his
Beak you can Judge a Woodcock', which were more
recent. Of these 'The Boy in the Bucket' is a most
beautiful story of a boy's irrational fear, the other
two laconic fables of odd and macabre events. Of the
eight stories in GOODBYE, WHAT WERE YOU? (1994) a
miscellany which includes poems, translations and
essays as well as stories, only 'The Golden Pony' was
newly collected.

Glyn Jones's COLLECTED SHORT STORIES, which the University of Wales Press has in preparation, will contain all the writer's work in this genre. It will be an event long awaited. To have the evidence of Glyn Jones's mastery of the short story in one volume will be a splendid, indeed essential, addition to Anglo-Welsh literature. He was certainly a master. His created world was probably restricted, although it gains in consistency because of this. The people it contains are complete and unexpected, like life. They give to his work a range and size that is wholly impressive. His style, too, is absolutely equal to his material. Lyrical, exuberant, poetic, rumbustious, exact, his prose is muscular and powerful or delicate or simple, as he needed it. The climate of the times was unfavourable for short stories when he first published them, otherwise he would have gained the attention he surely deserved. Not that it mattered very much to him. He was a modest man.

III

Do you know those marvellous words of Kant? 'Be a human being and treat everyone else as a human being'.

(Glyn Jones, in a letter, 25 October 1969)

That Glyn Jones moved from the short story to the novel seems logical in retrospect. His absorbed interest in human behaviour, his concern to present his characters in depth, the wealth of his literary talent, all suggest that the wide canvas of the novel would have tempted him. He was interested in the form from his early days as a writer, and wrote of himself that he had been influenced in different ways by *Melville, Joyce, Dylan, Lawrence, Whitman, Hopkins, Rimbaud, the 'Cywyddwyr', the authors of the 'hen benillion'*. And all these are representative of marked formal development, fascinating to a writer obsessed with his craft as Glyn Jones was.

There is further evidence, too, in the linked short stories, 'Bowen, Morgan and Williams' and 'The Water Music', with which he ended THE WATER MUSIC. His adolescent world had assumed so clear and vivid a presence that he could re-create it at will, and it is no surprise that two of his novels, THE VALLEY, THE CITY, THE VILLAGE (1956) and THE ISLAND OF APPLES (1965) drew heavily on this world, and continued, as it were, the last pages of THE WATER MUSIC. There is even some small proof that Glyn Jones thought that Wales ought to have produced a novelist or two: an anonymous reviewer reported him as saying,

What we need now is a few long-distance men – novelists and critics. But it's only a matter of time, isn't it? Wales is bound to produce a major prose-writer in English before long.
(SOUTH WALES MAGAZINE, Autumn 1970)

But to suggest so deliberate a reason is unrealistic; even the novels bear the marks of his typical method of composition, his paragraphs collecting around a phrase or image, as in his stories or poems, developing as a kind of organic growth. It is this, reflecting as it does an enviable wholeness of personality and a pure concern for the work, that made all Glyn Jones's writing, in whatever medium he cared to use, so much of a piece.

Glyn Jones wrote three novels. In addition to the two already mentioned he published THE LEARNING LARK in 1960. As in his other work, all three are set in Wales. They share, too, other properties; all are written in the first person, all depend boldly on Glyn Jones's own experience, all are concerned in one way or another with the world of childhood, although THE LEARNING LARK is less directly concerned with children than all the others. Much of the action in all three takes place in the Glamorgan valley in which Glyn Jones's Ystrad is to be found, that same town in which he set his earliest stories; all three are about contemporary characters, and are, indeed, concerned with time passing. This last factor means that in his novels Glyn Jones abandoned the old rural world which in his other work seemed to have little relevance to the twentieth century. His country stories seem to have happened long ago, perhaps in the last century, in some golden world of certainty and clarity. There are, it is true country passages in two of these novels, which are more leisurely, less stridently governed by time than the action of the towns; but there is no room for the marvellous old world in which, say, 'Wat Pantathro' was imagined. This perfect story of a faulty and pathetic universe made whole by a boy's love for his father, is triumphant is spite of its pathos, heroic in spite of the limitations of a boy's experience, huge despite its brevity. I take this to be one of the very best of Glyn Jones's stories. Yet in some ways it might have been easier to write such a story in that simpler environment. The novels, on the other hand, could almost have been designed to prove that, while worlds change, boys do not, that they remain sensitive, heroic, worldly, innocent and remarkable.

Though the three novels have much in common, they are also vastly different. If they share a south Wales background, they also occupy widely different countries of the mind, pose different problems, offer to us recognizably different human situations. Despite the smallness of his boundaries, Glyn Jones was not a regional writer. Nor is the fact that all three novels were written in the first person significant, except that it demonstrated Glyn Jones's absolute identification with the scenes and characters of his imagination. Such a complete involvement – although Glyn Jones had used his own life for some of the properties of his work – has led some critics to assume a much more autobiographical element than there is in his writing.

The problem of construction must have been a difficult one for so intuitive a writer, and it would seem that THE VALLEY, THE CITY, THE VILLAGE, Jones's first novel, has an almost imposed form. Episodic, written in a series of paragraphs loosely linked to each other, the novel is built in the three sections indicated by its title. It is, then, an ingenious development of the short-story writer's technique. The plot, if there is one, traces the growth from childhood of a young man born to be a painter, who recognizes his vocation early, but cannot admit it openly because of the most difficult of oppositions, that of a loving, and loved, older person who wants only what is best for the boy, but who cannot understand his need to paint. Both the boy and his wonderful grandmother, and their soft, affectionate confrontation, are made entirely credible; all is created from within.

Superficially the novel bears some resemblance to the early story 'I Was Born in the Ystrad Valley'; perhaps the little Trystan of the novel is the boy who was to grow up into the revolutionary young artist of the story, but such resemblances are not important. They indicate merely the depth of Glyn Jones's roots, and how, for every new work, he returned to his brightest memories.

However, if there is a suspicion that the construction of the novel was imposed, that it may have been a framework within which the writer could move the more confidently, this does not imply that there was any constriction on the abundance of Glyn Jones's style. (This, indeed, is the work which caused a number of reviewers to reach wide-eyed for their dictionaries and to comment, with admiration or despair according to their temperaments, on the unlikely words he poured before them.) Even within each section, even on successive pages, the style is very different:

Rosser's Row, to which my grandmother and my Uncle Hughie
had brought me to live, was a colliers' terrace, standing on the
bank of the black river oiling down the cwm. *The houses, very*
tall, four-storied in the backs which overlooked the river, were
built of bare grey shale with an occasional slab showing up
brightly ochreous; they were, to the rear at least, irregularly,
squarely, and minutely windowed, and here and there the whole
barrack-like structure was protected against subsidence by large
iron disks and rusty embossments bolted like cyclopean coinage
into the external walls.

So, in the first paragraph, the young man Trystan
depicts, paints, with his eye for pattern and colour,
the scabrous row in which he lived as a child. (It is
worth noting the importance of the black river,
'oiling' down the valley, in Glyn Jones's prose. We
have met it, clean enough to swim in, and singing
through 'The Water Music'; in this novel it is the focal
point of the scene, the one ever-present aspect of the
valley and the element which symbolizes the unlikely
cruelty of the striking miners in that appalling
passage in which the young men haul their blackleg
victim, roped, against the current; it is the same filthy
and miraculous water which kills the hero's father
and brings into his life the marvellous boy, Karl, in
THE ISLAND OF APPLES. It is the necessary and life-
giving water of the land of youth.) But such
deliberate and organized description, that of the
recalling artist, can change in a few paragraphs as
scene and character demand. When the boy Trystan is
playing truant with his friend Trefor, and the whole of
life is sharpened and heightened with adventure,
then the language is simple and carefree, and small
events are given the importance they seem to achieve:

When the school bell stopped ringing we found some soft tar on
the road and we walked about on that for a bit. Then we sat

34

down by the roadside where the kerb was high and watched the
people and the traffic. Trefor pulled half a plate of rhubarb tart
out from inside his shirt and we ate it between us. Sam the
baker's bread-cart passed very slowly and the front wheel went
over a big shining gob that we had seen Harri Barachaws, the
rag-and-bone man, spitting on the ground.

In these lines, by most artful re-creation, we share
the timeless experience of the little boy; he and his
friend walk about *for a bit*, the bread-cart passes *very*
slowly. We understand, too, that this is a very special
little boy, already looking at everything with the
detached curiosity of the artist. In these early pages
all experience is sensual, as it would be for a child.
Time is measured, if measured at all, by what is
visible, tangible, audible. And even in a neighbour-
ing paragraph, in which the child Trystan has given
way to his older, remembering self, it is just such
concrete detail which is recalled:

Often in her dim, sweet-smelling kitchen we sat as now by the
fire together, while she held her mangled hands heavily upon her
aproned knees. They were red and rugged, the hands of a
labourer, their knotted erubescence evidenced familiarity with
the roughest work, they seemed as though the coarse substances
at which they had laboured had become an element of their
conformation. Often, when I was older, and knew the meaning
of those bony and inflexible knuckles, the large, inflammatory
fingers, I turned my gaze from them with shame and pity . . .
Often I stared at those hands and remembered the way they
sought, in her bitter childhood, the warmth and comfort of her
pig's wash burden . . . Often, in winter, when the wind was
rough and cold on the bare mountain slopes, she rested with her
burden beside the steep path, and held for a moment her frozen
hands deep in the warm slop of a pig's food.

In this passage, the rhythms slow and heavy, the

rhetorical vocabulary ornate and eloquent, it is still the detail, palpable and real, that is evoked, the experienced life of a small boy. But such conscious rhetoric, although we have met it before (particularly in the long passage of praise in 'The Water Music'), is worth commenting on. Its subtle repetitions, its piling of image on image in sumptuous modification and redefinition, is very like that of the Welsh poetic convention known as *dyfalu*.

She did not wish to recall her childhood's struggles, the grim grammar of the school she had learnt in, instructing herself in loneliness, and in secret even, to read and write; she did not wish me to know how she had sat on her bed night after night, a simple Welsh book on the chair before her, and the shadows of the bars falling in candlelight across it as she tried to read. She did not wish me to know of the monotonous food, the cast-off clothing, the drudgery of that time, and then the encaustic history of her widowhood, her laundering, her chapel-cleaning, the endless sharing of her home with strangers . . .

There had been such women in Glyn Jones's family: his great-grandmother *taught herself to read Welsh and English*, his father's mother, coming from Goodwick in Pembrokeshire, took in the four orphan children of her brother and brought them up with her own children, just as the little Trystan was taken in by his grandmother after the death of his parents. Children in Glyn Jones's work are singularly unfortunate, or, as Wilde would have said, careless about their parents. The boy in 'Wat Pantathro' is motherless and his father a drunkard; Trystan is an orphan, his friend Trefor has no father; the seven O'Leary children *lived wild as bears and with no parents* in THE VALLEY, THE CITY, THE VILLAGE; Dewi Davies loses both parents and Karl Anthony never seems to have had any in

THE ISLAND OF APPLES. This gives to Glyn's children at once an extraordinary vulnerability and, when they need it, a great deal of independence. It means, too, that the love and warmth which Trystan receives from his Gran and his Uncle Hughie constitute a very special, a very privileged condition.

All this is clear in the beautiful first section of THE VALLEY, THE CITY, THE VILLAGE. It traces Trystan's life from the comfortable certainties of childhood to the probing doubts of adolescence; it shows us his despair when, because his grandmother does not understand his wish to paint and he is unable to agree with her ambition that he should become a preacher, he compromises and goes to university to train as a teacher. It includes a number of stories within stories, like the introduction of his aunts from Llansant, those messengers of hope from a better world. A number of typically remarkable Glyn Jones characters appear and disappear – the most memorable being the eccentric Anna Ninety-Houses – whose lovely talk shows us how acute and accurate was Glyn Jones's observation of his valley people:

But I met Maria Penrheol by the Greyhound and she said it was only a chill you had and there's bad that poor dab is looking, like a rush, and I didn't know her without her wens. I passed her, girl, not saying a word, 'There's proud you are,' Maria said to me, 'there's proud you are getting Anna Protheroe.'

After this almost self-contained section, we move to the city. This is where the university is situated. It is an unhappy place for Trystan:

When I had been in that place, Dinas, a fortnight, I still wondered what there was to like in it.

37

As far as Trystan is concerned, the place is inhuman, its houses designed to contain the dead; in a Dickensian passage, Glyn Jones describes the town in which Trystan was to live:

Over the bay window hung dreary chenille curtains of severe purple, approaching black, dividing a heavy penumbral gloom among its many corners. All the chairs and the window sofa were stained a tarry black and upholstered in unyielding and funereal mohair. The nigrescent table-cloth seemed cut from the same dismal material as the window-curtains but from a remnant of a dowdier and swarthier purpuration. The iron grate, the hob, and the mantelpiece, together with the fire-irons, had been indiscriminately stove-enamelled bv Miss Machen to a gloss of even and inhospitable black . . .

Understandably the inhabitants are strange and vulpine to a degree, and the students, perhaps in compensation, are frenetically active, often in anti-social ways. Even they, although lively and individual enough, are hardly orthodox in appear-ance:

And then Alcwyn came to stand by me. He was slim and spectacled, with wavy albino hair and a cast in his eye . . .

He also has invisible eyebrows and the corners of his mouth are unsteady, but nobody is ordinary in a Glyn Jones novel. It was part of his faith that nobody in the world is ordinary, and, by Dinas standards, Alcwyn is attractive enough. Here is Trystan's landlady, the glacial Miss Machen, the owner of the mausoleum described in the passage quoted above:

Her Sabbath-day dress was of some thick blackish material, very stiff, like tarpaulin or roofing felt, but wormed all over inch by

inch with intricate and silky black braid the thickness of tubular
boot laces. It had a high collar supported on whalebones under
her fig-like droppers, with narrow pleated lace showing its edge
against the tortoise neck-skin. On her mannish bosom, one
offering no glance-hold, featureless and inaccessible as a jail
wall to the sensual eye, hung a gold-framed cameo from a golden
lover's knot . . . Her bony ice-cold hands . . . were the large and
masterful graspers of a wicket-keeper . . .

The extraordinary fancy of the wicket-keeper's graspers is a typical touch. Jones's references were entirely his own, and his search for accuracy of metaphor and simile often led to a strange kind of scrupulous surrealism, of a physical habit, a habit of the imagination, something like that of the metaphysical poets without their hard intellectual content.

This is not to imply that 'The City' is just a gallery of marvellous portraits. This is the section in which Trystan makes friends, fails his examinations, attends an art school, until the university authorities stop him, and finds his romantic dreams of fair women brought up against lurching reality. And it is the section in which his grandmother dies. Like 'The Valley', it is written in short, episodic passages, each almost self-contained but combining to give an impressionistic account of an undergraduate's life. They do not pretend to literal truth, being partial, funny, introspective, biased, but they do add up to an understanding of Trystan Morgan which is complex, sensitive and unusually complete. It reminds one of some passages from Joyce's PORTRAIT OF THE ARTIST AS A YOUNG MAN, not only because both books take as their subject the full portrait of a young man, and not only because both writers used somewhat similar narrative techniques to do so. In both novels the movement is from the sensual experience of the child to the self-questioning interior life of the young man, and both Joyce and Glyn Jones used a similar episodic form. Again, Dedalus in A Portrait and Trystan Morgan in The Valley, the City, the Village are particularly sensitive, they are artists, knowingly aware of their solitariness in the midst of their friends, watchful and detached while seeming to take part in boisterous undergraduate behaviour.

In spite of the skill of this middle section, some of the essential tension leaves the work after the death of Trystan's grandmother. It is hard to retain interest in a situation which is clearly solved long before Trystan himself gets round to deciding that he will be a painter. We admire the understanding with which Jones described the uncertainties of the young artist, but the true dilemma has gone: in this sense, too, the last part of the novel, 'The Village', is a long epilogue rather than an integral part of the construction. However, it is in itself a technical accomplishment of some quality. It recounts Trystan's retreat, with his friends Nico and Gwydion, to Llansant. This is a recurrent pattern in Jones's work, and we may take it that Llansant is the thinly disguised Llansteffan in which he himself spent so many happy summers on his relatives' farm when he was a child. Certainly the confused Trystan needs some time there:

I came to Llansant as I never remember to have done before, hurt and still at times even despairing.

The place is full of healing presences, like his Uncle

Gomer whose *long and princely face* delights the painter's eye and whose sprawling stories beguile his mind; it is full, too, of healing time. In these last pages, the introspective young man remakes his world, explains to himself his disappointments, recognizes his failures.

The novel ends in a long interior monologue, a comic vision at once sincere and very amusing, in which Trystan on the edge of sleep, imagines a day of judgement in which his friends and his relatives are concerned, and his grandmother is judge. It is a memorable passage; if its purpose is to suggest that the past has been judged and that the morning is to bring a fresh and positive beginning – and this implied by the judge's comment *Every day is Judgement Day, Anna Bach* – then it succeeds.

The novel, then, has many important qualities, and for a first novel it was a remarkable achievement. It certainly deserved to be The Book Society Recommendation and earned its many favourable reviews. It probably fails to hang together completely; we remember scenes and certain events, but the central core is not as strong as its incidental strengths. What Glyn Jones revealed is that he was the master of the superb image, the sentence, the short paragraph. An anthology of the best short passages of English prose would have to contain any number of examples of his work. Again, the book is full of wonderful characters; but what had been a strength in the short stories – his drawing away from the tale to describe, in the fullest detail, some character who had wandered in – was in some measure a weakness in the novel. It held up the narrative far too much and too often, and the tendency was not helped by the fact that, having space in the novel, there was no need to sharpen the effect. It is not that the writing was self-indulgent. Glyn Jones was too delighted a craftsman to write like that, but that he sometimes enjoyed himself too much on relatively unimportant matters. What comes through most strongly, perhaps, is this sense of delight and enjoyment; there is a miraculous fund of creativity which runs throughout the novel, full of colour and prodigal of its strength.

THE LEARNING LARK was a very different matter. In some ways it is innocent of any of the guarded strictures I have made about THE VALLEY, THE CITY, THE VILLAGE. It is more coherently designed, its style is more uniform, its central theme is clearly defined. In all these ways it is a more successful novel. But it is also a much less ambitious novel, and the only work of Glyn Jones's maturity which may be said to have a purpose other than literary.

It is concerned with education, *concerned*, as the blurb says, *with current problems such as discipline, intelligence tests, eleven plus, the training and promotion of teachers, and so on* . . . and Glyn Jones's opinions on these matters are often put in the mouth of his hero, Johnny Thomas. Johnny is tremendous:

Johnny was a very big chap, over six feet in height, and if he had stood up straight, and if his bandy legs had been in proportion to his trunk, he would have been nearer seven feet . . . He was violent and lazy. In school he always lounged about, lolling against the classroom walls, and rolling from side to side in his slow prowl along the corridors . . . Johnny's face was anything but handsome. And yet you couldn't call him plain. The only word for him was ugly.

The 'I' of the story is not as dedicated a teacher as Johnny. He has no wish to become a headmaster, not even in Treniclas, that corrupt valley town where headships are obtained by political chicanery, by subtle flattery, by sufficiently large insurance payments to those members of the Education Committee who are insurance agents, and by membership of one of the Mafia-like families who run local affairs. But Johnny does, and the tale is the picaresque account of Johnny's journey to a headmaster's chair, through the sitting-rooms of the councillors where his honesty leads to some comic misunderstandings, through all the unorthodox and accepted machinery of promotions in Treniclas. That he ends, of course, by becoming the headmaster of Penn Street School, the school in which he is an assistant when we meet him, only by the intervention of true love, is Glyn Jones's sardonic comment on the situation. Johnny, honest and outspoken Johnny, marries into the right family and is promoted by the usual infamous methods in spite of himself.

The book, as might be expected, was a *succès de scandale*. The DAILY MAIL carried a nice feature in inch-high letters, *I AM SHOCKED BY THIS TAMMANY HALL*. The EMPIRE NEWS, which was later to serialize the story, told us that *It's a Job for the Boys Bombshell!* And other newspapers – the WESTERN MAIL, the SOUTH WALES ECHO and the MERTHYR EXPRESS perhaps the most obviously – commented more on the social aspect than on the literary side of the novel. In this they may have been right, because the novel has not worn well.

THE LEARNING LARK has many virtues. It is lively,

very funny, it is full of character – what P. N. Furbank in the LISTENER, called *a promising set of soaks and frauds and monomaniacs* – and the pace is fast and inventive. It displays Jones's splendid ear for valley talk:

'Right first time, Mr Thomas,' he said, 'Osbourne Summer-hayes. I thought you'd know me, sir, the boy who dropped the milk bottle out of the bell-room and nearly brained the care-taker. Remember? Missed him by inches. Old Fred, wasn't it? And remember the time I broke my leg falling off the woodwork roof and you took me home in a wheelbarrow? And when I was sick on the floor of the class-room after smoking? Remember that? You sent Nye Clark for a shovelful of ashes to put on it. And he brought hot ones. "What the hell are you trying to do, Nye, boy, fry it?" you said to him. Pity for Nye . . . '

and the plot is simple and effective. It is also the nearest thing to a fashionable novel that Glyn Jones has written.

On the debit side, Glyn Jones attacked (to quote Furbank again) *obvious and old-fashioned targets*. This was surely proved by the delight with which his 'revelation' of corruption was greeted on all sides. Everybody agreed with Glyn Jones; he made public what had been known for years, so that we all nodded our heads, aired our own examples of perfi-dious councillors and incompetent headmasters, were pleased and amused. Again, his attacks on the eleven-plus and intelligence tests, sound though they were, had been heard in schools and colleges throughout the country in 1960 when the book was published. Even Idris Parry, the most enthusiastic and knowledgeable of all Glyn Jones's critics, was moved to remark that *it sounds like an educational tract.*

44

It has more important and more surprising shortcomings. Johnny Thomas, to begin with, is almost too big a character for the story; this is not wrong in itself, but it makes the narrator a very shadowy figure indeed, a poor weak moon to Johnny's fulminating sun. He acts only insofar as he responds to Johnny's situations, he seems to have very little life of his own. One reads of his courtship with amazement and it is probable that the young lady is more determined than most or nothing would ever have come of the affair. Then there are nagging illogical circumstances, happily ignored in the pace of the narrative, but which niggle away afterwards. To begin with, Dewi Davies, our narrator, is himself part of the system, appointed in the time-honoured way:

> . . . after my mother had pulled a few wires in the shape of local councillors and ministers of religion, I got this teaching post as general subjects master at Pennsylvania Street Secondary Modern School . . .

He is an unlikely tilter at educational windmills, even in the company of Johnny Thomas. As far as Thomas is concerned, he is a *north* Walian and we are not told *how* he was appointed. It could not have been straight, that is certain; it must have been by error.

There is, too, an air of unreality in the writing itself, which is thrown into sharp relief when an event, completely irrelevant in its context but probably taken from Glyn Jones's own experience, is used:

> Eddie Hossington had been absent the day before . . . so I casually accused him of mitching. He went crimson with

45

indignation. 'Indeed to God, I didn't, sir,' he said. 'If I was to drop down dead by here, I didn't.' I was so taken aback I gave him the benefit of the doubt . . .

But the sincerity and innocent anger of the little boy stand out; it is a memorably authentic passage.

Alan Sillitoe, for whose opinion one must have great respect, reviewed THE LEARNING LARK on several occasions, never failing to say that the novel owed nothing to Kingsley Amis's LUCKY JIM. I agree with Sillitoe, yet there are interesting parallels between the two novels. Both are concerned with an educational system which allows incompetent and dishonest men to achieve positions of power and authority; both have as heroes ambitious young men who are determined to succeed; both young men do succeed through marriage into highly influential families; both novels have elements of high comedy and farce and both are set in south Wales. Johnny Thomas is both more honourable and less honest than Amis's Lucky Jim; he is, on the one hand, a dedicated teacher concerned to run an efficient and humane school, but on the other hand he does not see that he also needs power and that he is intolerant of ideas which differ from his own.

Glyn Jones was the last man to get publicly angry about anything, and it may be that the criticisms, implied and open, in THE LEARNING LARK are too good natured. Imagine what Smollett would have written about this set-up. (Smollett is a good name to mention here; he too liked to dwell on the physical appearances of his characters, drawing unlikely resemblances to animal and other inhuman properties; but what venom, what bitter anger, informs that work otherwise so much in the manner Glyn Jones used.)

Reading THE LEARNING LARK again, one is bound to agree with Idris Parry's opinion:

it shouldn't be any good at all. But it is. Mind you, I think it could be a lot better than it is. And I think it will be – the next time – with this experience in hand and this particular vendetta worked out of the system . . .

Prophetic words; the next time Glyn Jones published a novel it was the magical THE ISLAND OF APPLES, strange, unique, a masterpiece, surely the high point of his work. Glyn Jones wrote in a letter:

What sparked off 'The I. of A.', was the actual appearance in the Castle School of a boy who gave me, so many years later, the idea for Karl. Having been brought up in such a close community as Merthyr was in my schooldays, I was always fascinated by the appearance of any stranger from outside that community – 'Where did he come from?' I used to wonder. 'What sort of a place did he live in before?' 'What sort of friends did he have?' 'What sort of brothers and sisters did he have?' 'How did he dress?' Even 'what sort of weather did he have over there?' – wherever 'there' was. In THE VALLEY, THE CITY, THE VILLAGE there is a similar visitor, the character Gwydion (Dion) whose background is also quite different from that of the other students . . . When I was in about Form 3 of the Castle a boy turned up in Form 5 or 6, called something Angell . . . He was an aloof boy (he had to be, he had no friends in Merthyr), different, 'talking posh', and walking about Merthyr in the evenings wearing a sombrero. I invested him in my mind with all sorts of mystery and romance . . . The other man who supplied something to the conception of Karl was a chap I met in college, again an 'outsider', an exotic, different from the majority of the rather callow students in that dreadful place, a man of superior sophistication and experience obviously, again rather aloof and withdrawn . . . All this is background stuff and only important to the extent that it means that Karl was a real boy, he is supposed to exist . . .

THE ISLAND OF APPLES is concerned with Avalon, the island of youth. Its inhabitants are adolescents and a few adults whose lives impinge in some ways on those of the youngsters. It is an ordinary enough world, ribald, funny, inexplicably sensitive in the way of adolescence. Into this world comes Karl Anthony. He could not have appeared more dramatically:

The first time I saw Karl Anthony he was floating down past our house in the river.

So the story begins, and the lives of Jeffy Urquhart, Tom Griffiths Pugh, Charley Llewellyn and Dewi Davies are immediately made richer and stranger. (The links between all three novels, though slight, are nevertheless unmistakeable. Bowen, Morgan and Williams, those boys from THE WATER MUSIC, link the short stories to THE VALLEY, THE CITY, THE VILLAGE; Dewi Davies, the amiable narrator of THE LEARNING LARK, bears the same name as the narrator of THE ISLAND OF APPLES; there are strong resemblances between Trystan Morgan in the first novel and Dewi Davies in the last. Similarly, THE VALLEY, THE CITY, THE VILLAGE and THE ISLAND OF APPLES are both constructed in three sections.)

This novel, like all true works of art, grows bigger with time. In it Glyn Jones created a real voice for his narrator, absolutely alive, absolutely consistent, a speaking voice human enough to make literary and artificial the convention used by Salinger in THE

48

CATCHER IN THE RYE. Again, he makes the group of local boys so complete, so rounded, so recognizable, that Karl Anthony, the exotic newcomer, appears all the stranger, almost unreal in some ways. All Glyn Jones's marvellous freshness and sensuousness of detail are displayed here, all the loving particularity with which he saw the physical individuality of his people. He wrote, as I have said, like a Smollett whose motivation was not disgust, but love; in this novel his exuberant fancy rarely led him to dehumanize his characters in his search for the exact simile. This is a world of the finest observation and equally unusual imagination. On the one hand are the local boys, Jeffy, Tom and Charley, living the intensely detailed and full lives such children lead, while having only peripheral interest in and knowledge of events only a few yards outside their senses. They live in the real world, firm, clear and palpable. But Karl Anthony is much less tangible. About him lies mystery, tragedy and a glamour which is at once beautiful and menacing. The link between them is Dewi Davies. We see everything through his eyes, his is the recording voice which makes his friends understandable, and the new-comer – because Dewi does not understand him and because he is in need of a figure who can create miracles – mysterious.

Dewi Davies is a splendid creation. Sensitive beyond the ordinary, full of instinctive self-knowledge (he knows, for example, that the rash on his stomach has a psychotic origin and recognizes its symptoms with resignation after he has been excited or upset), marvellously observant, possessed of an inclusive memory, neurotic, he is the true citizen of Afallon, that strange place in which the real and the imagined are hardly to be distinguished. He is, too, at a very difficult stage of his development. He has lived a very sheltered, rather comfortable life; his family is comfortably off, his house is not one of a huddle of identical cottages in a miners' row, he exists in his own small island within the general island of youth which is the novel's title. This security is broken by the entrance of Karl Anthony. Indirectly, since Dewi's father dies as a result of an illness caught from the filthy river when he rescues Karl, the strange boy causes the first tragic event in Dewi's life. Soon, Dewi's mother dies, and the boy is another of Glyn Jones's orphans. In the midst of what would seem to be overwhelming circumstances, Dewi shows little sorrow. His main reaction is one of pleasure that the death of his parents has resulted in his living in the same house as Karl Anthony.

In contrast to the detailed description lavished on the other characters, Dewi tells us little of Karl. We know that he is elegant and very fair; in this he is the complete opposite of Dewi's father, who had been short, fat, hairy and very ugly. Dewi makes of Karl a father-substitute, and, because he knows (even if he does not admit it to himself) that he is in real danger, that is he realizes that adolescence is a brief and threatened time, he also invests the boy with magical ability. Apart from being noble, of high birth, mysteriously wealthy, handsome, proud, secretive – all of which Karl may really have been – Dewi persuades himself that Karl can right all wrongs, destroy the adult world which threatens his own, be perfect in arrogance and beauty, protect Dewi in an unbreakable safety of brotherhood. He can confound authority without difficulty or concern, he is apparently indifferent to the praise of other people. To Dewi he is D'Artagnan at first, and later almost a god in his divinity. Some of his exploits take place in clear daylight, in circumstances which are explicable and credible; in one of these he acts as spokesman for the whole school when the boys were aggrieved at learning that all other schools in the town had been closed owing to an outbreak of typhoid fever. (Such an incident actually took place during Glyn Jones's own schooldays.)

Karl, then, we may assume exists on two planes. He is an attractive and mysterious boy to whom Dewi is drawn; he is also, at another level, Dewi's own creation. In compensation for his own weakness, Dewi gives to his imagined Karl all the vivid powers which exist only within himself, and for long periods he is unable to distinguish between reality and fantasy. It is significant that he is an only child, and it is likely that Karl is almost the imaginary playmate invented by younger solitary children for their comfort. At a particularly horrible period of his life, Dewi's comfort lies in Karl's invulnerability. Karl is aloof, determined, self-sufficient except, thrillingly, for his need for Dewi's friendship; his activities are destructive and antisocial, ending in arson and murder. Such anarchic behaviour seems to be a compensation for the restrictions of Dewi's own world, and a fantastic interpretation of those demonic forces which are often strongest during adolescence, those urges which tempt boys to destroy the world and re-create it in an ideal form, acceptable to them.

If we accept this as a reading of the novel, then we recognize the curious alternation between the clarity and logic of reality, symbolized perhaps by the boys who are Dewi's long-term friends (it is noticeable that they are not nearly as keen on Karl, and seem never to be about for the more unlikely or 'imagined' adventures), and the equally clear and precise, but dream-like, episodes in which only Dewi and Karl are involved.

Dewi's confusion of reality and imagination is almost complete at times. Karl is a great romancer; his tales, full of stock properties, noble and mysterious birth, islands in the sun, Gothic castles, the menace of discreet strangers always at the edge of sight, are continued in Dewi's own dreams. Again, it is odd that Dewi should fall asleep when Karl relates these tales, preferring the attractions of his own romances.

The novel, then, is a fantasy, a psychological novel of a boy's torment as he struggles through a time which would have been too much for him to accept at once. There is some evidence that Dewi uses his idea of Karl as an aid to his own growing up. He may not be able to face the whole of reality, but certain aspects of his own personality, his fear of heights for example, worry him, make him ashamed. In a fine piece of bravura writing, Karl tells the boys of his climb to the top of a great tower, the remains of a railway viaduct which had once crossed the valley. It is so complete an account, so beautifully realized, that it reads like one of the great climbs. Handhold and foothold are minutely described, and so are the tremendous moments when the boy hangs two hundred feet above the sleeping valley. He becomes almost a surrogate for Dewi. The whole experience of climbing, the effect of height, are made real for him. In so many ways, he makes Karl do his living for him.

And this, perhaps, is the achievement of THE ISLAND OF APPLES. The hero is not Karl Anthony, but little, sad, stubborn Dewi Davies, who waits until he is strong enough to take the world on its own terms, who knows his brief shimmering childhood is coming to an end and that the weather is going to be bleak and grey. When he is ready for such knowledge he gets rid of Karl. In a mad, apocalyptic flight from the grown world (supposedly because Karl has been accused of the murder of Growler, the sadistic – or merely grown-up – headmaster), Karl and Dewi reach the estuary. In the midst of the storm Karl steals a yacht and, unable to pick up Dewi who is waiting for him on shore, sails on. His yacht is dismantled and wrecked and Karl drowned:

When it was over the steamer hooted far out, and in her beam when the lightning stopped, I caught sight of Karl floating rapidly on the current, his body rising and falling on the surface of the water as the flood carried him towards the sea. Soon he would be past me, and gone forever into the darkness . . .

So Karl leaves as he had entered, floating unconscious in the river, and the boy Dewi is left safe on land, realizing that his 'pursuers' were also his 'rescuers'.

The brambles held me fast although I struggled, and in the lamps of my pursuers I saw the green rain falling cold, my rescuers had landed from the steamer and were in the woods all round me.

Such a storm, such a constructed 'death' in a dream,

is psychologically and artistically the only way in which Dewi can return to the real world.

In a most sensitive review (in the OBSERVER, 4 April 1965), Irving Wardle clearly recognized the unusual quality of THE ISLAND OF APPLES. In it he wrote of *the sustained act of the imagination* which had been necessary for such a book, and then added:

The theme is the departure of youth, and Mr Jones has translated it into despairing action and marvellous natural imagery which convey, as strongly as I have ever experienced it, the sense of loss. Here is the authentic voice of the knight on the cold hill-side: the dream of the unattainable caught at the moment before it fades.

This is high praise, but thoroughly just and accurate. The novel was republished by the University of Wales Press in 1992, with a distinguished Introduction by Belinda Humfrey.

THE ISLAND OF APPLES is full of the most subtle allegory and symbolism, the texture firm and bright. Glyn Jones created a living world, and then an imagined world within that, an act of high imagination matched by a technical virtuosity both tactful and unobtrusive. As far as I know it is unlike any other novel, although the theme of lost youth is one of the most common in literature. Some critics have compared it to Alain-Fournier's LE GRAND MEAULNES. This to me is a meaningless exercise, since the two are so unlike. Glyn Jones's novel has none of the golden nostalgia of the French work, nor is it a love story; it is sturdy, often amusing, poetic in quite another way. It is the last, the most complete, the most surprising chronicle of the Ystrad Valley.

IV

. . . and I've written a few more poems. Two new ones are in John Stuart Williams's anthology POEMS '69 *and one in the new* OUTPOSTS. *I don't know how good they are. I like doing them more than anything anyway . . .*
(Glyn Jones, in a letter, 23 August 1969)

There is no doubt that, despite his work in the novel and the short story, Glyn Jones thought of himself as first and foremost a poet. He began as a poet, and was still at work on his long poem, 'Seven Keys to Shaderdom', near the end of his life. That the University of Wales Press was about to publish his COLLECTED POEMS gave Glyn great pleasure and satisfaction, and it was disappointing that he died before this important volume appeared. It arrived in 1996, meticulously edited by Meic Stephens, the accompanying Notes themselves fascinating, and with the advantage of an interesting Introduction by Mercer Simpson, another of Jones's friends. Friendship was also an art long practised by Glyn Jones.

To have a lifetime's verse in one volume allows us the inestimable opportunity to examine as a whole the work which Glyn Jones thought his most important, liked *doing more than anything anyway*, and to which, as writer, reader, translator and chronicler, he largely dedicated his life.

In his lifetime Glyn Jones published only three

collections of verse. The first, simply entitled POEMS, came from the Fortune Press in 1939, when he was twenty-eight. He was a late starter – twenty-five when his first true poems were written. But he soon broke into print, three of his poems appearing in the DUBLIN MAGAZINE in 1931. Seamus O'Sullivan, editor of the DUBLIN MAGAZINE, was sympathetic to the work of young Anglo-Welsh writers as well as quick to recognize real ability, for not only did he accept Glyn Jones's poems *with some enthusiasm*, but he was the first editor to take work from Alun Lewis and R. S. Thomas. One of Glyn Jones's poems which appeared in O'Sullivan's magazine was *a sixty-five line long piece of blank verse . . . called 'Maelog the Eremite' which described the musings of a hermit who occupied a cell in Gelli Faelog, near Merthyr . . .* This poem was diminished to an imagist excerpt of eleven lines and called 'Linnet' when it appeared in Glyn Jones's second collection of poems, THE DREAM OF JAKE HOPKINS (1954). Both versions are included in the COLLECTED POEMS, however. The poet's third collection entirely of poetry was SELECTED POEMS (1975).

The long period, nearly fifteen years, between the publication of his two books of poems had always been a difficulty when considering Jones's verse. Even after the publication of SELECTED POEMS, most of which were already published pieces anyway, only a handful of later poems had appeared, some in journals. The miscellaneous collection SELECTED POEMS: FRAGMENTS AND FICTIONS (1988), which included eighteen new poems, was evidence, however, that Jones continued to be faithful to his old craft. Even so, his output seemed relatively small for so long a career.

Yet looked at another way there is much more of it than one might have thought, for all his work, in whatever medium, has the quality of poetry. We have seen how easily a prose passage of his belied its printed appearance and came happily out in its true colours from the pen of Hugh MacDiarmid as the poem 'Perfect' – a title, just and accurate though it is, which Glyn Jones would have been too unassuming to adopt. It is a matter of some regret that the piece continues to be included in MacDiarmid's volumes.

Jones's method of composition, too, has always been the same for both poetry and prose. It was not unlike that used (if 'used' is the right word) by Dylan Thomas. Both poets seem to have begun with an image, a phrase or two 'given' as it were by some external power, and built on that. Glyn Jones was explicit on this point:

A poem for me is a structure. When I hear critics praising a poet because he 'probes into the deepest recesses of the modern consciousness' or 'expresses in a unique way' this that or the other, I lose interest . . .

(Glyn Jones, in a letter, 23 October 1971)

He saw himself as *a 'maker', rather than a 'seer', or a 'prophet', or a 'thinker'.* In this he was like Robert Graves, who wrote in the 'Foreword' to his POEMS 1970–72:

The word 'poetry' meant in Greek 'the act of making' – a sense that has survived in the old Scottish word for a poet, namely 'maker', though the Scots often spell it 'makur'.

Glyn Jones was very well aware of this attitude, even as a young man. In the most interesting 'Sketch of the Author', a series of prose notes in which he explained his practice and summarized his work up to that time (it concludes the POEMS of 1939, but is only selectively quoted in the COLLECTED POEMS), he tells us that his poems are *built up solid out of concrete nouns*. It is a remarkable document in that it demonstrates the unusual degree of self-under-standing Glyn Jones had reached at this early stage of his career. He was quite aware of the nature of his gifts and the direction in which he was to develop them; indeed, the 'Sketch of the Author' anticipated certain qualities not at that time apparent but which appeared more strongly later. It also made clear the relationship of his work to that of his great exemplars.

For in this, too, the work in prose and poetry is at one. Just as the influence of Lawrence is to be seen in the early prose, so it is evident in some of the early poetry. Just as there was a significant change in style of the stories after the meeting with Dylan Thomas in 1934, so we are able to see what a releasing influence this had on Glyn Jones's poems. The POEMS of 1939 is still an exhilarating book, reflecting a young man's excitement in the discovery of poetry, the realization that he was himself a poet; it is full of the spirit of those times.

Glyn Jones was one of the band of young poets who signed on eagerly under the banner of Keidrych Rhys's WALES, one of a company which included Dylan Thomas, Vernon Watkins, Peter Hellings and Keidrych Rhys himself. Idris Davies appeared in those pages, as well as poets from outside Wales, such as George Barker. Later THE WELSH REVIEW was to publish work by these and other young Welsh writers, as under the editorship of Professor Gwyn Jones this magazine offered them another platform. In some ways, the POEMS of 1939 is almost an expression of those days since WALES lasted for eleven issues between 1937 and 1939, ceasing to exist (although it had a brief life later) because of the outbreak of war.

Generally, what has been said of the prose might almost be repeated about the poetry; but there are other and important things to say. We can accept that the poetry and prose are closely related. We can make a case for considering all the prose, with the exception of THE DRAGON HAS TWO TONGUES, as poetry in that it relies for its genesis on something like inspiration, is maintained by techniques more normally used in poetry, and makes unusual use of the power of imagery and rhythm.

POEMS certainly shows that old dichotomy between town and country, and this time in a rather different way. It reveals something that we might have expected, that by nature Glyn Jones was not a dweller in towns, but in villages. The thirty-one poems in the collection are each distinguished by their place of origin. (This is a convention which Meic Stephens has discarded in the relevant section of COLLECTED POEMS.) 'Gold', for example, was written at, or connected with, Penrhyn Gŵyr, 'Rain' at Dinas, 'Easter' at the Gower, and so on. Cardiff does not appear as the location for any poem, despite Glyn Jones's residence in that city, although Roath and Tiger Bay are named. These areas, of course, were distinctive and self-contained communities, villages in their own right. Llandaff, in which Glyn Jones lived, is very properly called 'the village' by its inhabitants. We have seen in the stories that no town is bigger than Merthyr Tydfil, a town in which it was possible to know almost everyone, and that Cardiff is again never mentioned, except in passing, as Caerdaf. It is significant that in THE VALLEY, THE CITY, THE VILLAGE it is the village that is the place of refuge, the happy place.

Part of the attraction of Dylan Thomas's poetry, as with that of Lawrence, may be that they both use natural imagery, and this may also explain in some measure Glyn Jones's admiration for the work of Hopkins. It is probably part of the reason for his recognition of the qualities of the *cywyddwyr*. Even more likely is the early influence of the nineteenth-century poems that Glyn Jones found in Palgrave's GOLDEN TREASURY, the verse of the Romantic poets and their followers, for whom the natural scene was an essential source for their imagery and indeed their created worlds. Late in his life Jones remembered clearly the intoxication of his discovery of these poets and could quote them at length.

The Lawrence parallel is a significant one here. Miners were marvellously fierce in their enjoyment of nature. Often they were very knowledgeable amateur naturalists, great gardeners and skilful breeders of small animals and birds. Glyn Jones could not help but be influenced by such an environment, just as Lawrence had been by his mining village. It is not strange that a poet born and bred in Merthyr Tydfil should also celebrate so instinctively the peace of small communities and the natural splendour in which they exist. He was very properly the poet of such places, and of the mysterious fringes of the areas where town and country meet. He loved, too, the people who live in such communities and his admiration was unbounded for people who make their own villages wherever they are: for his father, who would ignore the traffic in Queen Street, Cardiff, and, with a peremptory wave of his stick, walk indomitably across the road as if he faced no more than a baker's cart. Or for Huw Menai:

More than once on Thursday afternoons, when the excursion trains brought the shoppers swarming from the mining valleys into the centre of Cardiff, I noticed there a tall, spare, large-boned figure, well over six feet in height, walking bare-headed the busy streets of the city . . . That was indeed Huw as he kinged it among the swarms of his dumpier fellow country men . . .

There seems to be a huge delight in that passage, as a man shows the folly of the great city, the natural stability and humanity of the village.

This was not necessarily obvious in POEMS when it first appeared, although it seems so now. It was a young man's book, eager, experimental, ardent. Like every young man's book, it paid tribute to those poets the author admired; what is unusual is that Glyn Jones knew this:

I started off powerfully under the influence of D. H. Lawrence. By this I mean (is it necessary to say it?) that the vocabulary and imagery of Lawrence affected me deeply when I first encountered them, but that I remained entirely indifferent to the Lawrence doctrine. I was delighted with the brilliance of his colouring, with the richly sensuous texture of his verse and so on, and like most young poets I tried to reproduce in my own early poetry the effects I admired. But I don't care much for the derivative verse I wrote in that early uprush of expression . . .

I met a famous young poet, a countryman of mine. His verse seemed to me to entirely disregard the reader, or the potential reader, of whose existence, because of my socialist theories, I had always been acutely aware. But paradoxically this poet who appeared completely unconcerned with the social or communal aspect of poetry, was also the one for whose work . . . I felt the greatest admiration at the time. We argued, and . . . partly in relief . . . I dismissed the figures of the young collier and the engine-driver and the coal-trimmers from my mind and summoned there in substitution the familiar images . . . from the mirror-maze.

. . . Many of the pieces I wrote at that time arose directly from contact with Welsh folk stanzas . . .

This was extraordinarily clear-sighted self-criticism, particularly from a young writer so near his 'early poetry'. We should not be deceived by the artful distancing of such phrases as *that early uprush of expression,* or *when I first encountered them,* or *at that time.* All those quotations come from the 'Sketch of the Author' in POEMS, and Glyn Jones had been writing poetry for all of eight years! This was real confidence, justified by the inclusion among his 'early poetry' of a number of poems that nobody but Glyn Jones could have written, by the realization that he had found his own voice.

Simply then, there is a group of poems which show, in greater or lesser measure, the influence of Lawrence. Among these I would put 'Gold', 'Meeting' and 'Esyllt', three poems which Glyn Jones himself acknowledged as Lawrentian. To these I would add 'Return', 'Rain' and 'Marwnad'. The first three reflect Lawrence's *brilliance of colouring* and the *richly sensuous texture of his verse* – the more immediately attractive of his qualities:

> *A midday half-moon slopes in heaven, tipped*
> *And empty, with her golden liquor spilt.*
> *She rolls transparent on the floor of heaven.*
> *She has splashed her wine of gold upon the broom*
> *And poured it over golden chain adrip*
> *With honey-drench . . .*

('Gold')

The last are more reminiscent of Lawrence's 'Nottingham miner' poems, those in which he described, usually from the woman's point of view, an incident from daily life, often connected with accidents in the colliery. The shape of these simple poems is almost like those of the Caroline poets, or perhaps like those in Joyce's CHAMBER MUSIC. This suggests that Lawrence had influenced the young Glyn Jones in deeper and more subtle ways than he himself might have realized. The only fully realized women in Jones's fiction, for example, tend to be the old, powerful, warm and comfortable grannies; young women are sketched in and soon vanish from the scene, so these girls whose husbands die in the pits:

> *My cheeks are dry for you, my man,*
> *   But you know what's for me –*
> *Even now I am wondering when my pains –*
> *   Will come upon me . . .*

('Marwnad')

or who wait with insensitive lovers in the wet:

> *Here in the dripping darkness*
> *   Under the trees,*
> *My cheeks might not be burning*
> *   For all he sees . . .*

('Rain')

are surely sisters to the women in Lawrence's poems, or even their shadows.

There are also the poems which owe something to the excited recognition Glyn Jones gave to the work of that *famous young poet, a countryman of mine,* Dylan Thomas. These include 'Sande' –

> *Sande's crucifix, that crisscross star.*
> *The risking saint, naked and upright, scans*
> *His crop of hills and prays against the dark . . .*

– as well as 'Easter', 'Rant', 'Man', 'Song' and 'Wounds'. Such definition is necessarily over-simplified since all these poems may bear evidence of other influences too – 'Esyllt', for example, has some interesting *cynghanedd*-like alliteration and 'Wounds' also shows something of Jones's reading of the Welsh medieval poets – and all are quite certainly the poems of Glyn Jones. But some echo of Dylan Thomas's voice is to be heard in, say, 'Easter':

> *No stick of light bulls on the useless lids;*
> *Spittles for the stony bread of living dried*
> *In these, who rode a skidding wheel, or sat*
> *Receiving at the eyes . . .*

Enough to demonstrate that Glyn Jones had also decided, at times anyway, *to entirely disregard the reader.*

There are a few simple, ballad-like poems ('History' is an example) in a vein which Glyn Jones did not explore, and an interesting group of poems in which he used sound-patterns drawn from Welsh poetry to attain a verse-texture not unlike that of Hopkins:

But
Behind the cape day's great sun hits the sea;
Rain greys two blue bays; his flesh his plumes
Flame-flushed, the burning gull flees bearing fast
Fire, flashed out, launched across the flooded east;
Blush-feathered, frocked, above the grey-bled sea
He bears my beating heart with rosy webs . . .

('Gull')

or more successfully:

The smudged west badged with Venus, then the moon,
One bare black beech leaf-skeletoned against
Her unsunned marigolden light, borne low
Over Merthyr like a cripple. Mayday;
The thrush, the throaty blackbird, ball-bounce and perch.

('Tree')

Others in this group might include 'Shadow' and 'Wounds', but there are examples of the style in almost every poem:

I recoil confronted by the menace
Of the gathering stars. They stand out
In brilliance from their ambush, one by one –
Surrounded I surrender.

('Stars')

There remain those poems which are complete and realized, owing little of their quality to anyone else, standing elegantly on their own merits. The first of these is 'Scene', a poem immediately recognized as Jones's, looking forward as it does in its confident sweep, its wide visual setting, its typical mixture of grandeur and humour, its curious imagery which combines with meticulous accuracy the natural and

the industrial, to the superb 'Merthyr', included in
THE DREAM OF JAKE HOPKINS. Here is a typical Glyn
Jones opening passage:

This is the scene, let me unload my tongue.
The north swells bunioned with Pumlumon whose
Side leaks water like some rusty old
Boiler's brickwork; his bleedings plait; cars at spring-tides
Line the river roads, switch headlights on, stroke
The stopped tide with car-beams, finger the night bore.
That's Severn. Southward, beyond the bottled Channel,
England, Somerset, like foreign parts, and west
John Masefield's notchy water, Cardigan Bay.

Here, from the height of his beloved Brecon Beacons,
Glyn Jones looked down on Wales. It was his
unchanging standpoint, in his work and his life. He
was at one with the gulls and soaring birds that
inhabit his poems, far-sighted, relishing his vision.
He could see the whole of Wales, speak to all her
people:

You men who bus or walk for mart-day towns,
Bear baskets full containing fish or rabbits,
Are river limers, clubbers of salmon,
I might have been and liked it, born like you
Westward, or north beyond the crooked coalfields.

But night on the valleys and my first star stands
Voluble above those Beacon peaks
Gesticulating like a tick-tack man.

('Scene')

The success of this fine poem and others like it –
'Ship', 'Dock', 'Choirs', 'Island' and 'Town' for
example – shows just how far Jones had progressed

in a few years. These wonderfully confident poems, all the result of personal experience and direct observation, were certainly *built up solid out of concrete nouns*. Some of them show the young Jones as a poet of his time as well as a poet of Wales. In these lines we hear the tone of 'thirties poetry', suggesting that he was well aware of what his contemporaries, Auden, Spender and Day Lewis, were doing elsewhere:

> *Now she begins to stand in from the Roads, and*
> *To set herself slowly towards the open caisson,*
> *Putting her black prow in delicately between*
> *The dreadful dockwalls, with the juddering siren*
> *Fastened at her funnel-front spouting back*
> *Thick steam . . .*

('Ship')

This group, together with the section entitled 'Biography', represent some very accomplished writing. The striking arrangement in 'The Slum-World' (one of the sections from 'Biography') reflects also Glyn Jones's abiding interest in painting; they have the effect of a painting by Braque or Chagall:

> *The horn gramaphone, the tumbling pigeons, two*
> *   rosy blue-eyed*
> *Fish-heads pointed in a stinking kiss, and the solo*
> *   road*
> *Rejoiced like a dance-dress down its tape of*
> *   sunlight.*
> *Here he went guided through the governed squalor*
> *   of his world.*

The strength of POEMS, then, lay in what had been seen, organized and experienced. The best work is admirably sure-footed, ambitious in scope, full of muscular writing. Its weaknesses lie in the poems, like the lines spoken by bereaved young women, where the poet, while sympathetic to the situation, has insufficient experience to deal with it. They are fictional and not fully realized. POEMS was the work of a young man, a very promising young man, poised one would have thought for a splendid career.

The COLLECTED POEMS includes in an Appendix a substantial group of 'Imitations and Early Poems', some of them not necessarily inferior to those in POEMS, some of them obviously prentice work. They are evidence of the amount of poetry Jones was writing during the years up to 1939, and one would have expected another collection to follow POEMS within a short time. But it was fifteen years before THE DREAM OF JAKE HOPKINS appeared.

We can only guess at the reason for so long a silence. Certainly Glyn Jones was deeply affected personally and professionally by the outbreak of war in 1939. Probably he was influenced by the sudden end of WALES, the magazine which had brought him into contact with so many other writers and which had given him the encouragement necessary for a young artist's development. Perhaps, too, the demands of his job as a teacher, were more exhausting than many people realize, particularly as for periods during the war he had to travel long distances to the schools in which he taught. *Why do you want to become a teacher?* Dewi Davies was asked in THE LEARNING LARK:

It was no good saying you liked the short hours and long holidays. The answer they wanted from somebody like me was:

'For the last six years I have been engaged in the work of destruction. Now I want to have the chance to do something constructive in my life.'

Hardly a born teacher, Dewi. But for Glyn Jones the situation was heavily ironical. He cared about his boys, he worried because he was only a *conscientious* teacher, he was often too tired to write after the day's work. In a note he claimed that teaching is *in many ways a good job for a writer* and that he always withdrew from other possible employment *because the job always threatened to take up more of my time and energy than teaching.* Even so, there were times *when I found it exhausting and often I could do nothing at night except watch television.* Again, he saw many of his contemporaries lead irresponsible and bohemian lives, of which he disapproved – but not on moral grounds.

I often think it a pity writing has got mixed up with bohemi-anism, another time-waster. Few Welsh language writers (any?) have been real bohemians. The circumstances here are different. Wallace Stevens, T. S. Eliot, William Carlos Williams – these managed to combine a career with poetry.

(Glyn Jones, in a letter)

But very few teachers are able to write as much as they would wish, perhaps because the job is so concerned with words, with communication, and many poems get lost as the teacher talks his way through the problems of others – in itself a kind of low-key poetry. Poetry is an act of the highest creative intensity. It may be that Glyn Jones was able to employ his creativity and his poetic gifts substantially in his stories and novels, the long labour of such work being paradoxically less exhausting than the final draining demands for perfection made by the poem. Jones, a painstaking craftsman, invariably went through many drafts before he was finished with a poem.

Whatever the reasons, THE DREAM OF JAKE HOPKINS was not published until 1954. The title poem has some bearing on our last paragraphs, based as it is on the life of an intelligent, sensitive and disappointed teacher. This is in no sense a self-portrait, but a long poem written for broadcasting in which Glyn Jones very sensibly dramatized a scene he knew very well. It is direct, simple and vigorous, employs a variety of verse forms and a number of voices, and, since it makes its meaning immediately clear and has colour and humour, must have made very successful broadcast material. This was Jones's aim.

. . . I tried to show Jake Hopkins first as schoolmaster, second as person and last as member of a community, commented upon by neighbours, colleagues, friends, etc. But whatever aspect of him I had to present I tried to make the picture clear, sharp, journalistic, to be apprehended immediately.
(Glyn Jones, in a note appended to THE DREAM OF JAKE HOPKINS)

He was notably successful in this. The poem has clear relationship to his novel THE LEARNING LARK and is often very like it. It may not be the most successful poem in the new collection, and one's interest is bound to be concentrated on those lyrics which were written after the completion of POEMS. They are immediately recognizable. The consistent bursts of song, the energy, the gusto even, the invigorating language, the shining imagery, all are present. The voice is the same voice we had heard in 'Scene'; but there are also striking advances. What had seemed artful and literary in 'Marwnad' is firm, tender and true compassion in 'Easter'. This poem is concerned with an old woman, dying while fine weather, *the honey-months*, transforms the world outside her bedroom, the world of the watching young:

> *In death's stink now, with tears I watch her, old*
> *And hideous in her dying – bitterly*
> *She moans, her face death-dark, her tangled hair*
> *Tortured behind her little rolling head . . .*

The poet can do no more, and no less, than reassure himself with the promise of resurrection of the renewed world, with the defeat of death:

> *Soon over grooved fields shall grow the soft*
> *Plush-pile of the grass-like wheat, the green*
> *Velvety nap of springing corn burst forth –*
> *Soon, soon, the doors of every grave shall open*
> *And the light of dawn shall shine upon the dead.*

That eloquent prophecy contains some of Jones's typical images: *the soft / Plush-pile of the grass-like wheat* and *the green / Velvety nap* of the corn, for example. He often compared the natural to the man-made in this manner. Typical, too, is the heightened and incantatory quality of the language. It can be found in many places, as in 'Cwmcelyn', one of the best poems he ever wrote:

> *His wings blissful in a silent drumming*
> *Of beautiful sunlight, the buzzard. Below him*

The estuary; below him the hills,
    Green hills with the hay gone; the cornfields,
    Silent and sunburnt encampments
Of wheat-stooks; below him the tranquil
River, gently heaving the mirrors
    Afloat on her surface; below him
    These woods, where flashes the grey pigeon,
White in the paint of her flying.
Below him Cwmcelyn, the farm.

The grey pigeon,/ White in the paint of her flying – what an image, the sort of thing he does again and again, bringing us up short with a sudden shock of delighted recognition, the visible world made larger and brighter for us. Both 'Easter' and 'Cwmcelyn' also showed that Jones's work had developed in other ways. His handling of the verse itself, his manipulation of complex verse forms, was by this time masterly. His mature skills enabled him to use deeper and more sombre tones. He had need for this. His vision was no longer blithe and sunny. He was aware of the reality of death and the common and painful imperfections of mankind. In 'Cwmcelyn' the buzzard, even with his perfect sight, cannot see, aloft in his beautiful and savage world,

    . . . the griefs of that homestead . . .
    Drunken,in anger, or passion,
    Dejected, trampling this warm web-work of shadow
        Between village and farm . . .

nor can he understand that, for the men and women of the farm,

    . . . Defilement was theirs, and folly,
        Suffering, questioning and death . . .

Such understanding is the poet's, and here are the first manifestations of a quiet and profound melancholy which was to underlie Jones's work from this time on. He mourned for *The soul's dissonance, and the despair*, not always as openly as in 'Cwmcelyn', but often recognizably. It was the source of the compassion for humanity, individually and generally, that ruled his outlook.

'Cwmcelyn' is also an example of the way in which Jones had often worked in his poetry almost from the beginning. He looked at his world from a height and took a long view from that position before detailing the particulars of his vision. He had done this in 'Scene' and other early poems, and did it again in 'Merthyr'. What was new is that the descriptive passages in his best work, the natural beauty he celebrated, are integrated into the poems, often opposing the darker content of human existence which follows, allowing him to come to a final meditative conclusion. He wrote such passages in abstract terms, using such concepts as 'folly', 'annihilation', 'dissonance', 'despair'. The manner is precisely that of Wordsworth in 'Lines Written a few Miles Above Tintern Abbey', or some of Coleridge's 'conversation' poems. Jones no longer wrote his poems completely in *concrete nouns*. He had come a long way, and perhaps fifteen years was not too long to wait.

'Merthyr', which is a much happier poem, employs rather similar methods. It is full of beautiful detail and warmed by the unquestioning concern for humanity that lies behind almost everything Glyn Jones wrote. It begins with a brief invocation in which the poet pleads,

> *Lord, when they kill me, let the job be thorough*
> *And carried out behind that county borough*
> *Known as Merthyr, in Glamorganshire.*

and moves on to a splendid description of the Brecon Beacons, a place known to Jones from boyhood:

> *It would be best if it could happen, Sir,*
> *Upon some great roof, some Beacon slope*
> *Those monstrous clouds of childhood slid their soap*
> *Snouts over, into the valley. The season,*
> *Sir, for shooting, summer; and love the reason.*

One can see at once that this is a jocular poem, very funny, poking sly humour at what is most admired in a way that is typically Welsh and which has disconcerted many an uncomfortable English reader. It is written in a marvellously natural reconstruction of the living voice, its relaxed couplets running on, and a lively varied rhythm talking over the iambic groundbeat. And having taken us to that *great roof* the poet had to show us all his treasury:

> *On that hill, varnished in the glazing tide*
> *Of evening, stand me, with the petrified*
> *Plantations, the long blue spoonful of the lake,*
> *The gold, stook-tufted acres without break*
> *Below me, and the distant corduroy*
> *Glass of the river . . .*

He took the exigencies of the rhyme in his stride, as marvellous opportunities to use inventions like the *petrified / Plantations* and *the distant corduroy / Glass of the river* rather than as difficulties to be surmounted. And then, from this affectionate grandeur, he brings us back to earth:

74

These are also the boys, *crippled Philip . . . rowdiest hunchback goalie in the game, squat Russ, Mr Jones the Stoning,* his wife in her *drake-head-green gown, her broad-brimmed hat . . .* Now, *All are dead . . .* Grateful for his memories, the poet asks God to bless them all, then realizes:

God bless the beautiful flats also, I suppose.
Lights go on in houses. People live in them . . .

and he unites the living and the dead in his final tender lines:

And great stars flash among vanished branches
And night-owls call from elms no longer there.

The definite intervention of the poet, in his own right, among the figures of the past, *the legendary/ Walkers and actors of it,* this is new; and so is the rhythm, easy yet firm, of the poem, allowing the thought to dictate its shape. The poem is typical of a number of beautiful pieces in which Glyn Jones celebrated his past and the people of his world. They are golden elegies, written with a quiet authority. One such is 'Nant Ceri', which I saw in manuscript before its publication. It is quoted in full.

Blessèd were those Bowens who saw all this – viz.,
   Dawn's sort of rosin glow, then the sun's red-gold
   Mountain, floating up through green, a dazzle
   In windows distant from this window; masses
   Of garden azaleas bloom plum-blue, porcelain
   Apricot, or their liquor, from emerald
   Fogs under the iron pear boughs, glows ruby
   Like jewels or lit wine; the long-tailed mountain pony,
   Milky, saddled with morning silver, wax-white
   On fire-green turf her unshod hooves, munches

In this hush of mountains her black rug
Of shadow; breeze blows the green grass blaze glossy
And bends, bows into a gentle curve, the children's
Rope, hung from branches of the flashing orchards;
A green moon too clouds milky as sea-glass –
Blessèd were those Bowens who saw all this
For three lifetimes and believed in God.

Of this *tour de force*, which calls to mind Glyn Jones's earlier manner in the catalogue of shimmering images and unites it with his celebration of the friends who also represent all humanity, the poet had this to say:

'Bro Ceri' seems to have become 'Nant Ceri' now. The poem started outside the back window in 'Brynhyfryd', the house we stayed in at Llanarth – the azaleas and the pear; a pony I saw up there in Cards., somewhere, invaded the scene, but the rope was actually in Llanarth; walking by the Ceri with D.J. (John Elwyn's brother-in-law), I had one of those sudden feelings of great happiness and I thought – how marvellous to live here, as D.J. and his family have done, and to have, like them, belief. All this, the eclectic scene, the happiness, the idea of belief, all suddenly, somehow, seemed to belong together . . . I spent many happy hours trying to get it right.
(Glyn Jones, in a letter, 11 September 1971)

(Nant Ceri is the lovely small river which enters the Teifi near Cwmcou, below Newcastle Emlyn. John Elwyn, the painter who was Jones's close friend, is a native of Newcastle Emlyn. His work appears on the covers of some of Glyn Jones's books and of those of other Welsh writers.)

Perhaps most remarkable of the poems in SELECTED POEMS is 'The Common Path'. Here all is muted and dark, the careful arrangement of observed details precluding the existence of the glittering images which had been so evident in Glyn Jones's verse. The tone is conversational, almost flat:

> *On one side the hedge, on the other the brook.*
> *Each afternoon I passed, unnoticed,*
> *The middle-aged schoolmistress, grey-haired,*
> *Gay, loving, who went home along the path.*
>
> *That spring she walked briskly, carrying her bag*
> *With the long ledger, the ruler, the catkin twigs,*
> *Two excited little girls from her class*
> *Chattering around their smiling teacher.*

The quiet, slow verse would be ordinary if it were not held together by a curious unease, a net of nervousness, of foreboding anticipation. Certainly the poet, although he has observed the woman carefully, did not find her an attractive figure; he was almost unaware of her as a human being:

> *I, free, white, gentile, born neither*
> *Dwarf nor idiot, passed her by, drawing in*
> *The skirts of my satisfaction, on the other side.*

All this is cleverly and tactfully done, the hint of biblical language reminding us obliquely of our Christian duty, of the parable of the Good Samaritan,

> *Her whole face kindled into life. I heard*
> *From large brown eyes a blare of terror, anguished*
> *Supplication, her cry of doom, death, despair.*

The poet *felt at once repelled, affronted by her suffering,* but was not surprised when he learned that, soon, the middle-aged schoolmistress was dead of *private,*

81

middle-aged, rectal cancer. His conclusion, in which he condemns himself for his lack of compassion, is very fine:

> *What I remember, and twenty years have*
>   *Never expiated, is that my impatience,*
> *That one glance of my intolerance,*
>   *Rejected her, and so rejected*
> *All the sufferings of war, imprisonments,*
>   *Deformities, starvation, idiocy, old age –*
> *Because fortune, sunlight, meaningless success,*
>   *Comforted an instant what must not be comforted.*

In that lovely poem we heard completely new notes from Glyn Jones. Welsh poets have often been slow developers; or rather, however good they have been when young, they seem to retain the capacity for growth and change and development even into old age, a marvellous faculty forbidden to most English poets. This, I suspect, is because the poet is still honoured in Wales, even by those who never read a line: his place is assured, he is needed.

Whatever the reason, Glyn Jones wrote some remarkable poems among the seventeen pieces included in SELECTED POEMS: FRAGMENTS AND FICTIONS. The elegiac 'Remembering Alcwyn' and 'The Meaning of Fuchsias' are substantial achievements. The darker 'Suicide Note', the amused love with which Jones celebrated his Corgi, 'Siani', and the technically brilliant *cywydd* 'Thanks to John', demonstrate the range of his work. And even if some of the poems – 'Report, Aber '84' is one – are occasional poems, they are all for various reasons of great interest.

'Seven Keys to Shaderdom', placed at the end of this section of THE COLLECTED POEMS, is as far from being occasional as is possible. There is evidence that Jones had worked on this long poem for many years, and it remained unfinished at his death. Meic Stephens has organized this version partly from *those sections which had appeared in print and partly from the hundreds of MS work-sheets and TS drafts . . . found among the poet's papers.* It is a surprising work, narrative, of course, dramatic, using a variety of poetic forms, and speaking through the voice of an old, failed painter. The persona, Twm Shader, is clearly a Glyn Jones might-have-been, and the use of an *alter ego* allowed Jones to explore situations and emotions quite unlike those found anywhere else in his work. His view of the world had darkened as he grew older, and in conversation, while still forgiving of individuals, was harsh about the world in general. It is in 'Shader' that he was able to speak out in judgement against the world in which he found himself living and his condemnation is unrelenting. Shader, whose memory is very like that of Glyn Jones, can lament the passing of the great beauties of Wales:

> *Where is Tangwen now, where Nest, where is Gwenllian,*
> *The apple-blossom and the summer's glow?*
> *Where are the 'gentle, gold-torqued maidens*
> *Of this island'? Where is Elen of the Hosts?*

But he moves, too, among:

> *. . . hostile foreign journalists, television crews,*
> *Rhyme-jaggers, daubers, bloused-out homosexuals,*
> *Sharpers, boozers, clods, pornographers,*
> *Churls, louts, fornicators, roués, debauchees . . .*

And, he at the end, *cowers, mumbling in the darkness.*

It is the most startling and impassioned statement of Glyn Jones's stark vision of the world. It is too early to comment on this extraordinary work, except to remark on its furious energy, and to recognize that it is also a statement of its opposition to the celebratory, almost ecstatic lyricism we saw in some of Glyn Jones's lyrics. And though the poems end with a terrifying vision,

> *We are sick and defeated, all are abandoned,*
> *with tears on our cheeks*
> *And with great weights heavy on our hearts.*
>
> ('Envoi')

it is also the necessary vision of the dark side of the moon.

V

All that remains now is to pay tribute to certain other aspects of Glyn Jones's work, for he wrote widely outside the poems, short stories and novels already discussed. His literary activities included radio and television scripts, some of them in Welsh, and he was a frequent broadcaster. Not only did he, in the field of translation, make *some of the few viable, unpoeticised translations of the great Dafydd ap Gwilym* (THE CONCISE ENCYCLOPAEDIA OF MODERN WORLD LITERATURE is my authority), but in collaboration with T. J. Morgan he was responsible for the beautiful Golden Cockerel Press version of THE SAGA OF LLYWARCH THE OLD (1955). There are, too, his translated selections of 'Stanzas for the Harp', published by Gwasg Gregynog in limited editions, and the 'Hen Benillion', English versions of which were included in GOODBYE, WHAT WERE YOU?, a miscellaneous volume of selected writings published by Gomer in 1994. He reviewed almost every writer of note who can be called Anglo-Welsh, beginning with a review of a novel by Rhys Davies in the very first issue of WALES in 1937. In his reviews he made acute, thoughtful and generous comments on writers as different as Idris Davies and Raymond Garlick, Geraint Goodwin and Emyr Humphreys, Dylan Thomas and Jack Jones.

His almost professional interest in painting, and his wide knowledge of art in general, found expression in a number of notices of important exhibitions. This was an early activity, for his review, 'Thoughts on the Burne-Jones Exhibition' appeared in THE WELSH OUTLOOK in 1933. In 1937 his article on Surrealism was published in TIR NEWYDD, a Welsh-language little magazine which lived briefly between 1935 and 1939. He retained throughout his life an active interest in all the arts.

His libretto for the opera, 'The Beach of Falesa', for which the Welsh composer Alun Hoddinott wrote the music, was published by the Oxford University Press in 1974, and was performed in the same year by the Welsh Opera Company. The libretto was based on a short story by R. L. Stevenson, by a happy coincidence the same story for which Dylan Thomas wrote a film treatment.

But by far Jones's most substantial achievement in what might be termed a field of secondary creativity must be THE DRAGON HAS TWO TONGUES (1968). At once personal and objective, this is a book that only Glyn Jones could have written. Composed, as the sub-title has it, of 'Essays on Anglo-Welsh Writers and Writing', it is not nearly as orthodox as this suggests. Scholarly, yet warm and human, authoritative but not over-serious, it remains a most valuable source-book as well as revealing, as does all his work, Glyn Jones's infectious sincerity and honesty of vision. He arranged the work so that he dealt first with an account of his own background, relating it to the situation of Anglo-Welsh writing in general, and suggesting causes and reasons for what may have been general resemblances in authors superficially very different. This most interesting first section, containing as it does a portrait of Merthyr Tydfil at an important stage of its history, is followed by a general introduction to short stories and novels and then a discussion of three prose writers: Caradoc Evans, Jack Jones and Gwyn Thomas. The unifying factor, and one which links the section with the previous pages is that Glyn Jones knew his men well, and personal knowledge and experience made the book not a collection of essays but a complete whole, much more than the sum of its parts. The same is true, and the same framework used, for the discussion of Anglo-Welsh poetry, this time his individual writers being Huw Menai, Idris Davies and Dylan Thomas. The great strength of the book is that Glyn Jones knew his material intimately, he was there. He was himself an important part of the exciting and invigorating explosion of talent which took place in 1937 or thereabouts and he remained both a watchful observer and a leading figure afterwards. His memoir of Dylan Thomas is the most authentic we have. The book is now out of print, but it is to be hoped that renewed interest in Glyn Jones's work will result in its being reissued. It is certainly needed.

Apart from its value as a precise record of a particular period in the history of Anglo-Welsh literature, THE DRAGON HAS TWO TONGUES has the incidental qualities we had grown to expect in Glyn Jones's work. It is beautifully written of course, its prose easy and relaxed, urbane and kindly, often moving to description as typically felicitous as any in the stories or novels:

Watching one day, not long before his death, the grave progress of Huw Menai across a Rhondda Street, the tall, gaunt figure, still erect at seventy-three, the pallid Eryri-rugged features, the imperious long-legged 'Kaffir' stride, I felt sharply the lack of some accompanying pageantry, of some poetic sodality or mysterious urdd, *strangely and hieratically clad, to follow in attendance upon him. But his only follower, at a distance of three or four yards, and trotting to keep up with him, was an undersized Welsh novelist . . .*

The book is also wonderfully generous to his friends without hiding any of their shortcomings. Perhaps the essays on Dylan Thomas and Jack Jones are the most delightful, and it may be that, of the six writers Glyn Jones treated in detail, these happened to be the most remarkable characters, the one a young man remembered in his youth, the other a man at the end of a career which, as far as writing was concerned, did not begin until he was fifty. In PROFILES, 'An Account of Welsh and English Language Writers in Wales today' (1980) we have Jones's opinions on the work of more recent writers, evidence if any were needed of his countinued concern with the state of English literature in Wales and for the younger men and women who were producing it.

Glyn Jones was not only for nearly sixty years a famous Anglo-Welsh writer, an exemplar and inspiration to younger writers, but also one of the best-informed and most clear-sighted critics. His deep engagement with literature never faltered over a career which spanned the publication of Keidrych Rhys's anthology MODERN WELSH POETRY (1944), THE LILTING HOUSE, the definitive anthology of Anglo-Welsh poetry edited by John Stuart Williams and Meic Stephens (1969) and the supplementary anthologies which have appeared since, in which his poems were included. He grew with the years from *the nice, handsome young man with no vices* of Dylan Thomas's letter to Pamela Hansford Johnson (11

May 1934, SELECTED LETTERS OF DYLAN THOMAS) until at his death he was the acknowledged doyen of Anglo-Welsh literature.

During his lifetime, despite its recognition by established critics, his work probably did not receive the widespread acknowledgement it deserves, although it was, and is, very obviously valued by his peers. He took with characteristic modesty the honours that came his way; he was the first Chairman and later President of the English-language section of Yr Academi Gymreig, and he was honoured in many ways by the Welsh Arts Council. In 1974 the University of Wales awarded him the degree of D.Litt., of which he was very proud; in 1988 he was inducted into Gorsedd Beirdd Ynys Prydain, and wore the White Robe of that company, and five years later he was made an Honorary Fellow of Trinity College, Carmarthen. In recent years, as interest is growing in the field of Anglo-Welsh writing and the schools and universities are actively teaching and researching in this study, young scholars are taking particular interest in Jones's *œuvre*, and young writers are excited by his mastery. His work will be with us for a long time.

Glyn Jones was a remarkable man. He would have been notable for his personal qualities if he had never written a line. He and his wife Doreen, to whom all his books are dedicated, made their home in Whitchurch a warm centre of hospitality and culture. He never lost his delighted curiosity about the vagaries of human behaviour, and was totally interested in the people he met on any chance encounter. He died at home in 1995, and is buried at

Llansteffan, the village he had known and loved since childhood, his country haven. His grave is marked by a plain stone, carrying his name, the years of his birth and death, and the single word of his profession, 'Llenor', or 'Man of Letters'.

Select Bibliography

Poems (collections)

POEMS, Fortune Press, 1939.

THE DREAM OF JAKE HOPKINS, Fortune Press, 1954.

SELECTED POEMS, Gomer, 1975.

COLLECTED POEMS, University of Wales Press, 1996.

Short stories (collections)

THE BLUE BED, Jonathan Cape, 1937.
        another edition, Dutton, 1937.

THE WATER MUSIC, Routledge, 1944.

SELECTED SHORT STORIES, J. M. Dent, 1971.

WELSH HEIRS, Gomer, 1977.

Novels

THE VALLEY, THE CITY, THE VILLAGE, J. M. Dent, 1956.

THE LEARNING LARK, J. M. Dent, 1960.

THE ISLAND OF APPLES, J. M. Dent, 1965.
        another edition, Day, 1965.
        another edition, University of Wales Press,
        1992.

Miscellaneous collections (prose and verse)

SELECTED POEMS: FRAGMENTS AND FICTIONS, Poetry Wales Press, 1988.

GOODBYE, WHAT WERE YOU? Gomer Press, 1994.

Essays

THE DRAGON HAS TWO TONGUES, J. M. Dent, 1968.

Translations

With T. J. Morgan, THE SAGA OF LLYWARCH THE OLD, Golden Cockerel Press, 1955.

WHEN THE ROSEBUSH BRINGS FORTH APPLES, Gwasg Gregynog, 1980.

HONEYDEW ON THE WORMWOOD, Gwasg Gregynog, 1984.

Criticism of Glyn Jones's work

In G. Grigson (ed.), THE CONCISE ENCYCLOPAEDIA OF MODERN WORLD LITERATURE, 1963.

'The Poetry of Glyn Jones' by J. S. Williams, in THE ANGLO-WELSH REVIEW, Vol. 16, No. 38, Winter 1967.

CONTEMPORARY POETS OF THE ENGLISH LANGUAGE, St James Press, 1970.

CONTEMPORARY NOVELISTS OF THE ENGLISH LANGUAGE, St James Press, 1972.

A special number of POETRY WALES, devoted to Glyn Jones's work, Vol. 19, No. 3. 1984.

Other works cited

Robert Graves, POEMS 1970–72, Cassell, 1972.

Gwyn Jones, 'Language, Style and the Anglo-Welsh', ESSAYS AND STUDIES 6 (1953).

Keidrych Rhys (ed.), MODERN WELSH POETRY, Faber, 1944.

John Stuart Williams and Meic Stephens (eds.), THE LILTING HOUSE, Dent and Christopher Davies, 1969.

Glyn Jones and John Rowlands (eds.), PROFILES, Gomer, 1980.

The Author

Leslie Norris was born in Merthyr Tydfil and educated at Georgetown School and Cyfarthfa Castle School. Subsequently he trained as a teacher at the City of Coventry Training College before taking the degree of M.Phil. at the University of Southampton, under the supervision of the poet F. T. Prince. He has taught since 1983 at Brigham Young University, Utah, where he is Humanities Professor of Creative Writing. He has contributed poems and stories to many magazines and anthologies on both sides of the Atlantic and has published collections of poetry and short fiction. His COLLECTED POEMS and COLLECTED STORIES were published by Seren in 1996. He has also written critical works on Edward Thomas and Vernon Watkins, among others. His many honours include the Katherine Mansfield Award, the Welsh Arts Council's Senior Award, the David Higham Memorial Prize, the Cholmondeley Poetry Award and the Alice Hunt Bartlett Prize. He is a Fellow of the Royal Society of Literature and of the Welsh Academy. He has received the degrees of Hon.D.Litt. from the University of Glamorgan and of Hon.D.Hum.Litt. from Brigham Young University. Professor James A. Davies has published an essential study of Norris's life and work which is included in this series (LESLIE NORRIS, Writers of Wales, University of Wales Press, 1991).

Designed by Jeff Clements
Typesetting at the University of Wales Press in
11pt Palatino and printed in Great Britain by
Dinefwr Press, Llandybïe, 1997

British Library Cataloguing in Publication Data.
A catalogue record for this book is available from the
British Library.

ISBN 0-7083-1410-4

The Publishers wish to acknowledge the financial
assistance of the Arts Council of Wales towards the cost
of producing this volume.